Homestyle
family favorites

Miss Lizzie's Pound
Cake, page 293

Homestyle
family favorites

Homestyle
family favorites

©2010 by Gooseberry Patch
600 London Road, Delaware, Ohio 43015
1-800-854-6673, **www.gooseberrypatch.com**
©2010 by Oxmoor House, Inc.
P.O. Box 360220, Des Moines, IA 50336-0220

Hardcover ISBN-13: 978-0-8487-3342-1
Hardcover ISBN-10: 0-8487-3342-8
Softcover ISBN-13: 978-0-8487-3343-8
Softcover ISBN-10: 0-8487-3343-6
Library of Congress Control Number: 2009937169
Printed in the United States of America
First Printing 2010

Oxmoor House, Inc.
VP, Publishing Director: Jim Childs
Editorial Director: Susan Payne Dobbs
Brand Manager: Terri Laschober Robertson
Senior Editor: Rebecca Brennan
Managing Editor: Laurie Herr

Gooseberry Patch Homestyle Family Favorites
Editor: Susan Hernandez Ray
Project Editor: Emily Chappell
Senior Designer: Melissa Jones Clark
Director, Test Kitchens: Elizabeth Tyler Austin
Assistant Director, Test Kitchens: Julie Christopher
Test Kitchens Professionals: Allison E. Cox, Julie Gunter,
    Kathleen Royal Phillips, Catherine Crowell Steele,
    Ashley T. Strickland
Photography Director: Jim Bathie
Senior Photo Stylist: Kay E. Clarke
Associate Photo Stylist: Katherine Eckert Coyne
Senior Production Manager: Greg A. Amason

Contributors
Editor: Kelly Hooper Troiano
Designer: Nancy Johnson
Copy Editor: Adrienne S. Davis
Proofreader: Jasmine Hodges
Interns: Georgia Dodge, Allison Sperando
Food Stylists: Margaret Dickey, Alyson Haynes,
    Telia Johnson, Ana Kelley, Connie Nash, Iris O'Brien,
    Angela Schmidt

Time Inc. Home Entertainment
Publisher: Richard Fraiman
General Manager: Steven Sandonato
Executive Director, Marketing Services: Carol Pittard
Executive Director, Retail and Special Sales: Tom Mifsud
Director, New Product Development: Peter Harper
Director, Publicity: Sydney Webber
Assistant Director, Newsstand Marketing: Laura Adam
Assistant Publishing Director, Brand Marketing: Joy Butts
Associate Counsel: Helen Wan

To order additional publications, call 1-800-765-6400.
For more books to enrich your life, visit **oxmoorhouse.com**
To search, savor and share thousands of recipes, visit **myrecipes.com**

Cover: Classic Baked Macaroni & Cheese (page 216)
Page 1: Crunchy Biscuit Chicken (page 55)

Dear Friend,

In today's busy world, there's just something comforting about foods rich with down-home goodness. Wholesome dishes that are shared at Sunday dinner, raved about at potluck gatherings, and passed down through generations warm the soul. Take a peek inside this keepsake collection at some of our favorites that are sure to strike a familiar chord.

Create memorable weeknight family meals with scrumptious recipes like Shepherd's Pie (page 71) and Callie Coe's Chicken & Dumplings (page 129). Rounding out dinner for your loved ones on busy evenings can be a snap with Mom's Squash Casserole (page 83) or Auntie Ruth's Potatoes (page 205). Or, gather everyone together for a heartwarming breakfast any day of the week. No-fuss favorites such as French Toast Croissants (page 87) or Sausage & Cheddar Grits (page 102) will be a hands-down winner every time.

We're also sharing warming soups, delicious sandwiches and melt-in-your-mouth breads...all tried & true recipes that are sure to please! And there's nothing more comforting than a little something sweet to end your meal. Satisfy your chocolate craving with Grandma's Chocolate Cake (page 298) or spend the afternoon baking a batch of Double Peanut Butter Cookies (page 269).

So flip through the pages...in addition to mouthwatering recipes, you'll find lots of how-to's and clever ideas for keeping meals easy and delicious. So whether you need a dish for a quick supper or special event, we hope this cookbook will be your guide.

From our families to yours,

Vickie & JoAnn

contents

Fried Chicken & Milk Gravy, page 127

Red Barn Chowder, page 191

Hot Fudge Brownie Sundaes, page 305

Kickin' Chili Fries, page 203

Pork & Raspberry
Sauce, page 37

celebration classics

If you're searching for that perfect dish for a bridal tea or ladies' luncheon, Tea Sandwiches (page 11), made with two types of cheese and a variety of herbs, are sure to satisfy partygoers. Celebrate Independence Day with a picnic featuring Grand Ma-Ma's Deviled Eggs (page 14) and Watermelon Slice Cookies (page 19). And for the big holiday feast, the tasty Roast Cornish Hens & Savory Rice (page 31) will bring smiles to the faces of your guests. Enjoy these and other scrumptious recipes to fit your special occasion.

Refreshing Mint Punch

(pictured on page 310)

With only 4 ingredients, this crowd-pleasing punch is easy to mix up.

2 c. fresh mint leaves, packed
2 c. water

12-oz. can frozen lemonade
1 qt. ginger ale

Bring mint and water to boil; bruise mint with potato masher. Set aside overnight; strain and discard solids. Add lemonade, 3 lemonade cans of water and ginger ale to mint mixture; mix well and serve. Serves 10 to 12.

Mary Murray
Mt. Vernon, OH

Cheese Straws

(pictured on page 310)

To make these addictive nibbles even more quickly, shred the cheese in the food processor before you begin.

2 c. all-purpose flour
2 c. shredded extra-sharp
   Cheddar cheese
1 t. baking powder

½ t. salt
6 T. ice water
1 c. butter, softened

Combine all ingredients in a food processor or heavy-duty mixer; chill. Roll out to ¼-inch thickness; cut into 2"x½" strips. Arrange on ungreased baking sheets; bake at 350 degrees for 10 to 12 minutes. Serves 4.

Judy Borecky
Escondido, CA

Tea Sandwiches

Fresh herbs and feta cheese make a terrific sandwich combination.

1 c. butter, softened
8-oz. pkg. cream cheese, softened
½ c. crumbled feta cheese
½ c. fresh parsley, chopped
1 T. fresh basil, chopped
1 T. fresh tarragon, chopped
1 T. fresh rosemary, chopped
salt and pepper to taste
12 to 16 thin slices wheat or
    oatmeal bread

Combine all ingredients except bread in a large mixing bowl; blend thoroughly. Spread desired amount of herb mixture over half of bread slices; cover sandwiches with remaining slices. Remove crusts; cut into desired shapes and chill one hour. Makes about 6 to 8 sandwiches.

Jo Ann
Gooseberry Patch

a portable herb garden

Tuck several herb plants inside a vintage tin picnic basket...so easy to carry to the kitchen when it's time to snip fresh herbs.

Ribs with Espresso Barbecue Sauce

The ribs and barbecue sauce can be prepared one day ahead. Just cool slightly, cover separately and refrigerate.

2 T. hot Mexican-style chili
    powder
1 T. paprika
1 T. ground cumin
1½ t. salt
¾ t. pepper
4 lbs. baby back pork ribs,
    cut into serving-size pieces

12-oz. bottle dark beer or
    beef broth
18-oz. bottle favorite
    barbecue sauce
½ c. water
2 T. brown sugar, packed
1 T. instant coffee granules

Whisk seasonings together in a small bowl to blend; rub mixture over ribs. Place ribs in a large heavy roasting pan and set aside. Bring beer to a boil in a large saucepan over medium heat; cook until reduced to one cup, about 5 minutes. Pour beer around ribs; cover tightly with aluminum foil. Bake at 400 degrees until fork-tender, about 1½ hours. Combine remaining ingredients in a saucepan over medium heat. Simmer until slightly thickened, stirring occasionally, about 10 minutes. Brush ribs with barbecue sauce; grill over medium-hot coals 3 minutes. Turn ribs; brush again with sauce and grill 3 to 4 more minutes or until thoroughly heated. Bring remaining sauce to a boil; serve with ribs. Serves 4 to 6.

Jo Ann
Gooseberry Patch

best basting

Using jute, bundle together fresh herbs such as thyme, sage or rosemary to create an herb basting brush…it really adds flavor to grilled foods.

Country Glazed Ham

(pictured on page 309)

Serve this ham on a large platter surrounded by whole cranberries and orange slice twists.

10- to 12-lb. fully cooked
    smoked ham, skin removed
    and fat trimmed

1 c. water
Glaze

Place ham in a shallow roasting pan and add water. Bake at 325 degrees for approximately 16 minutes per pound. If ham browns too quickly, place a tent of aluminum foil over it. Do not seal. When done, remove from oven and allow to cool. Spread Glaze over ham. Serves 15.

Glaze:

thinly sliced peels of 6 oranges
2 c. water
⅓ c. currant jelly

¾ c. orange marmalade
¼ c. red wine

Bring orange peels and water to a boil in a saucepan; boil 10 minutes. Drain; return orange peels to saucepan. Add jelly and marmalade to orange peels in saucepan and simmer 10 minutes. Remove from heat and stir in wine.

Juanita Williams
Jacksonville, OR

bowl full of fun

A yellowware bowl looks wonderful filled with fresh cedar sprigs and red apples!

Grand Ma-Ma's Deviled Eggs

The best method for boiling eggs is to place them in a single layer in a saucepan and add enough water to cover one inch above the eggs. Bring water to a boil; immediately cover pan and remove from heat. Let eggs sit, covered, 15 minutes. Drain the water and immediately place eggs under cold running water.

4 eggs, hard-boiled, peeled
   and halved
1½ t. vinegar
½ t. dry mustard
¼ t. salt

⅛ t. pepper
½ t. sugar
1½ T. butter, melted
¼ t. Worcestershire sauce
Garnish: paprika

Scoop egg yolks into a bowl. Arrange egg whites on a serving platter; set aside. Mash yolks well with a fork. Add remaining ingredients except paprika; mix well. Spoon into egg whites; sprinkle with paprika. Makes 8 servings.

Maureen Gillet
Manalapan, NJ

Country-Style Baked Potato Salad

A truly tasty salad…a spin on a loaded baked potato. Use any or all of your favorite toppings!

4 lbs. baking potatoes, peeled,
   cubed and cooked
1 lb. bacon, sliced into ½-inch
   pieces and crisply cooked
8-oz. pkg. shredded Cheddar
   cheese

½ c. butter, softened
½ c. green onions, chopped
1½ c. sour cream
1 t. salt
1 t. pepper

Combine all ingredients in a large bowl, tossing gently. Chill for 2 hours before serving. Serves 10 to 12.

Deanna Lyons
Gooseberry Patch

Classic Carrot Cake

Sprinkle cinnamon and chopped walnuts over the top of the cake...so pretty!

4 eggs
1¾ c. sugar
1 c. oil
2 c. all-purpose flour
2 t. baking soda
1 t. salt

1 t. cinnamon
1½ carrots, shredded
1 c. apple, cored, peeled and
    coarsely chopped
½ c. chopped walnuts
Cream Cheese Frosting

Blend together eggs, sugar and oil; set aside. Combine flour, baking soda, salt and cinnamon; mix into egg mixture. Stir in carrots, apple and walnuts; pour into 2 greased and floured 9" round baking pans. Bake at 350 degrees for 30 to 35 minutes or until a toothpick inserted in center comes out clean; cool on wire racks 10 minutes. Remove from pans; cool completely. Arrange one layer on a serving plate; frost with Cream Cheese Frosting. Add second layer; frost top and sides. Serves 10 to 12.

Cream Cheese Frosting:

8-oz. pkg. cream cheese,
    softened
½ c. butter, softened

2 t. vanilla extract
4½ to 5 c. powdered sugar

Blend together cream cheese, butter and vanilla in a mixing bowl with an electric mixer until fluffy; gradually mix in powdered sugar until smooth.

Janet Allen
Hauser, ID

Fourth of July Beans

It's just not summer without this favorite side dish!

1 lb. bacon, diced
1 lb. ground beef
1 lb. hot ground pork sausage
1 c. onion, chopped
28-oz. can pork & beans
15-oz. can ranch-style beans
15-oz. can maple-flavored
   baked beans
16-oz. can kidney beans,
   drained and rinsed

½ c. barbecue sauce
½ c. catsup
½ c. brown sugar, packed
1 T. mustard
2 T. molasses
1 t. salt
½ t. chili powder

In a large Dutch oven over medium-high heat, cook bacon until crisp; drain, remove and set aside. Cook beef, sausage and onion until meat is browned; drain. Transfer to a greased disposable aluminum roasting pan. Stir in bacon and remaining ingredients; mix well. Cover and bake at 350 degrees for 45 minutes. Uncover and bake for 15 more minutes. Serves 10 to 12.

Laurie Lightfoot
Hawthorne, NV

Watermelon Slice Cookies

These red and green treats are sure to be a hit at any summertime get-together.

¾ c. butter, softened
¾ c. sugar
1 egg
½ t. almond extract
2 c. all-purpose flour
¼ t. baking powder

½ t. salt
red and green gel food
   coloring
⅓ c. mini semi-sweet
   chocolate chips
1 t. sesame seed

Blend butter and sugar in a large mixing bowl at medium speed with an electric mixer. Beat in egg and extract; set aside. Combine flour, baking powder and salt; gradually add to butter mixture. Set aside one cup dough. Tint remaining 1⅓ cups dough with red food coloring and shape into a 3½-inch-long log; wrap in plastic wrap. Tint ⅓ cup reserved dough with green food coloring; wrap in plastic wrap. Wrap remaining plain dough and refrigerate all 3 doughs 2 hours or until firm. On a lightly floured surface, roll plain dough into an 8"x3½" rectangle. Place red dough log on the end of one short side of rectangle; roll up.

Roll green dough into a 10"x3½" rectangle. Place red-and-white dough log on the end of one short side of rectangle; roll up. Wrap in plastic wrap; refrigerate overnight. Unwrap and cut into 36 (1-inch-thick) slices. Place 2 inches apart on ungreased baking sheets. Place chocolate chips and sesame seed on red part of dough to resemble watermelon seeds. Bake at 350 degrees for 9 to 11 minutes or until firm. Immediately slice cookies in half. Makes 3 dozen.

Kay Barg
Sandy, UT

tips:

1. Dust off excess flour between layers of dough.
2. Press dough layers so they stick together.
3. Roll out green dough on parchment paper and use it to support dough when wrapping.

Fresh Peach Ice Cream

This creamy recipe tastes very rich…brings back memories of summer on the farm. Garnish with fresh mint.

5 c. milk, divided
4 egg yolks
8 peaches, peeled, pitted and
    mashed
2 T. lemon juice

2½ T. vanilla extract
½ t. ground ginger
½ t. almond extract
2 (14-oz.) cans sweetened
    condensed milk

Combine 2½ cups milk and egg yolks in a heavy saucepan and whisk well. Cook and stir over medium heat about 10 minutes or until mixture will coat a spoon. (Do not overcook, or it will turn into scrambled eggs!) Combine egg mixture with remaining milk, peaches and all remaining ingredients in a large bowl and stir well. Cover and chill. Pour mixture into the freezer section of an ice cream freezer. Freeze according to manufacturer's directions. Spoon into a container with a tight-fitting lid and freeze one hour or until completely firm. Makes about 16 cups.

Caramel Apples

It's just not October without these chewy, sweet treats! Keep 'em around for snacks or hand them out as party favors during a fall festival.

2 (14-oz.) pkgs. caramels,
    unwrapped
1½ t. vanilla extract
2 T. water

9 wooden craft sticks
9 tart apples, washed and
    patted dry

Combine caramels, vanilla and water in a heavy saucepan; cook, stirring constantly, over medium heat until caramels melt. Cool slightly. Insert craft sticks into apples; dip apples in caramel mixture. Place on a buttered, wax paper-lined baking sheet; refrigerate until firm. Makes 9.

Perfect Pumpkin Pie

If you like a crisp pie crust, bake on a baking sheet in the lower third of the oven.

29-oz. can pumpkin
1 c. sugar
1¼ t. salt
1½ t. cinnamon
¾ t. ground ginger
½ t. nutmeg

4 eggs, beaten
1½ c. milk
1½ c. evaporated milk
¼ c. butter, melted
2 (9-inch) refrigerated pie crusts
1 egg white, beaten

Combine pumpkin, sugar, salt and spices. Add eggs, milks and butter; mix well and set aside. Place pie crusts in pie plates. Brush crusts with egg white; divide pumpkin mixture evenly between crusts. Bake at 450 degrees for 10 minutes. Reduce heat to 350 degrees; bake for 30 more minutes or until pumpkin filling is firm. Makes 2 pies; each serves 6 to 8.

Lois Bivens
Gooseberry Patch

My mother revised this from an old label recipe to make enough filling for 2 pies. It turns out creamy, custardy and just spicy enough.

Lois

pretty pies

To make your pies more decorative, roll out extra pie crust dough, cut with shaped mini cookie cutters and press onto the top crust before baking. Or bake the shapes on a baking sheet at 350 degrees until golden...a fun topper for any kind of creamy pie!

Candy Corn-Popcorn Balls

Full of popcorn and candy corn, this treat will be a hit! You'll need to work quickly to shape the balls, so gather everyone to help.

2 c. sugar
1 c. corn syrup
½ t. cream of tartar
1 T. butter

½ t. baking soda
6 qts. popped popcorn
1 to 1½ c. candy corn

Heat first 4 ingredients in a heavy saucepan to 270 degrees on a candy thermometer (hard ball stage); remove from heat. Carefully stir in baking soda. Pour over popped popcorn; toss to coat. When just cool enough to handle, mix in candy corn and form into 3-inch balls using buttered hands. Set aside to cool completely. Wrap individually in plastic wrap or cellophane; store in an airtight container. Makes 16 balls.

Megan Tkacik
New Castle, PA

Delicious popcorn balls sweetened with candy corn!

Megan

party favors

Package treats, such as candied nuts, fudge, almond brittle, cookies, or brownies in airtight containers and then slip them into gift bags tied with ribbon or raffia. Set them in a basket by your door so there will always be a treat waiting for guests to take home.

Thanksgiving Crab Soup

Present this tasty soup with cornbread to keep everyone happy until dinner is served. Make the cornbread the night before and start the soup early Thanksgiving morning. It's ready by lunchtime and the tradition begins!

6 c. water
30-oz. can beef broth
2½ t. seafood seasoning
¼ c. onion, chopped
16-oz. can whole tomatoes

20-oz. pkg. frozen mixed vegetables
5 c. potatoes, peeled and sliced
16-oz. can crabmeat

Combine water, broth, seasoning and onion in a stockpot and bring to a boil. Add vegetables and simmer 1½ hours. Add crabmeat and simmer 1½ more hours. Serves 6 to 8.

Monica Vitkay
Bairdford, PA

Tangy Tomato Aspic Salad

Sprinkle a teaspoon of blue cheese crumbles on top of each serving for extra tang! This recipe is easily doubled to serve eight.

1½ c. tomato juice, divided
3-oz. pkg. lemon gelatin mix
½ c. mild salsa

shredded lettuce
½ c. sour cream
2 T. cucumber, chopped

Bring one cup tomato juice to a boil in a saucepan over medium heat. Add gelatin mix, stirring to dissolve. Stir in remaining tomato juice and salsa; mix well. Pour into a deep 6"x6" airtight container. Refrigerate until firm. Slice into 4 servings. Place each slice on a bed of shredded lettuce. Combine sour cream and cucumber; spoon dressing over aspic. Serves 4.

Bill Weedman, Jr.
Algoma, WI

Cornbread Dressing

Fresh cornbread crumbs and poultry make this homestyle dressing extra yummy!

3-lb. chicken
4 c. water
½ c. margarine, melted
1 t. salt, divided
1 t. pepper, divided
6 cubes chicken bouillon
4 c. cornbread, crumbled

1 c. celery, chopped
2 (10-oz.) tubes refrigerated
   buttermilk biscuits,
   baked and crumbled
1 c. onion, finely chopped
½ t. dried sage

Place chicken, water, margarine, ½ teaspoon salt, ½ teaspoon pepper and bouillon in a large Dutch oven. Cover and simmer over medium heat one hour or until chicken is tender. Remove chicken to a platter and let cool; reserve broth for dressing. Remove meat from chicken and chop into bite-size pieces. Place in a large bowl and set aside. In a separate bowl, mix together remaining ingredients with remaining salt and pepper. Slowly add cooled chicken broth to cornbread mixture until mixture reaches desired moistness. Gently stir in chicken; transfer to a greased 13"x9" baking pan. Bake, uncovered, at 325 degrees for 1 to 1½ hours or until golden. If dressing appears dry during baking, add extra broth. Makes 8 to 10 servings.

year-round Thanksgiving

Remind your family of all they have to be thankful for by serving this yummy dressing at different times throughout the year.

Country Butterscotch Yams

Country Butterscotch Yams

For an extra treat, top with half of a 16-ounce package of marshmallows and return to the oven until lightly browned.

8 (14-oz.) yams, peeled,
    cut into ½-inch slices
    and boiled
½ c. corn syrup
½ c. brown sugar, packed

¼ c. half-and-half
2 T. butter
½ t. salt
½ t. cinnamon

    Arrange yams in an ungreased 13"x9" baking pan; bake at 325 degrees for 15 minutes. Combine remaining ingredients in a 2-quart saucepan; boil 5 minutes, stirring constantly. Pour over yams; bake 15 more minutes, basting often. Serves 6.

Charlotte Weaver
Purcell, OK

Golden Potato Latkes

Enjoy these tasty potato pancakes the traditional way…topped with applesauce and a dollop of sour cream.

4 baking potatoes, peeled
1 onion
¼ c. all-purpose flour
4 eggs, beaten

1 t. salt
½ t. pepper
¾ c. oil

    Shred potatoes and onion in a food processor; transfer to a large bowl. Stir in flour, eggs, salt and pepper until blended. Heat oil in a large skillet over medium-high heat. Drop potato mixture into hot oil, 2 tablespoons at a time. Cook over medium-high heat, turning once, until golden. Drain on paper towels; serve warm. Makes about 4 dozen.

Irene Robinson
Cincinnati, OH

Noodle Kugel

Hundreds of years ago, cooks in Germany replaced the bread and flour in this once-savory, traditional Jewish recipe with noodles. Later in Poland, sugar and raisins were added, making it more of a dessert dish. The cottage cheese and sour cream provide a custard-like consistency...yummy!

1-lb. container cottage cheese
1 c. sour cream
4 eggs
1 c. sugar

1 t. salt
2 t. lemon juice
16-oz. pkg. egg noodles
1 c. raisins

This is a traditional family dish served at all family weddings.

Liz

Combine first 6 ingredients in a blender. Blend until smooth and pour into a large mixing bowl. Cook noodles according to package directions and drain. Combine noodles and cottage cheese mixture; blend in raisins. Pour into a lightly greased 13"x9" baking pan and bake at 350 degrees for 45 to 50 minutes. Serves 8.

Liz Plotnick
Gooseberry Patch

table settings

Make your dining table romantic. Tie wispy bows of tulle or satin at the corners of your tablecloth. Drape the chairs in netting and tie a lace bow around each chair back.

Roast Cornish Hens & Savory Rice

You'll find this main dish ideal for a special occasion...yet easy enough for a casual weekend meal.

1⅓ c. chicken broth
½ c. long-cooking rice, uncooked
½ c. sliced mushrooms
¼ c. celery, chopped
2 T. onion, chopped

½ t. dried marjoram, divided
½ t. salt, divided
2 (20-oz.) frozen Cornish game hens, thawed
1 T. oil
pepper to taste

Combine broth, rice, mushrooms, celery, onion, ¼ teaspoon marjoram and ¼ teaspoon salt in an ungreased 13"x9" baking pan. Arrange hens on top of rice mixture; brush with oil. Sprinkle with pepper and remaining marjoram and salt. Cover and bake at 375 degrees for one hour. Uncover and bake for 25 to 35 more minutes or until juices run clear when hens are pierced with a fork. Serves 2.

Jo Ann
Gooseberry Patch

on the side

Salad bar veggies really add variety to meals for one or two...they come chopped and ready to use, too. Toss them with leftover roast chicken for a tasty dinner salad, or sizzle with roast pork for a zesty stir-fry. So convenient!

Easy Pumpkin Roll

This fall favorite is so pretty...and really is simple to make.

1 c. sugar
3 eggs, beaten
⅔ c. canned pumpkin
¾ c. biscuit baking mix
2 t. cinnamon
1 t. pumpkin pie spice
½ c. chopped pecans

1½ c. powdered sugar,
    divided
8-oz. pkg. cream cheese,
    softened
⅓ c. butter, softened
1 t. vanilla extract

Gradually add sugar to eggs; beat eggs and sugar at medium speed with an electric mixer 5 minutes. Add pumpkin, baking mix and spices. Spread pumpkin mixture evenly into a greased 15"x10" jelly-roll pan lined with greased wax paper. Sprinkle with pecans. Bake at 375 degrees for 13 to 15 minutes. Sift ½ cup powdered sugar into a 15"x10" rectangle on a clean dish towel. Turn cake onto the sugared towel; carefully peel off wax paper. Starting at narrow end, roll up cake and towel together and cool completely on a wire rack, seam-side down. Blend cream cheese and butter at medium speed with an electric mixer until creamy; add remaining powdered sugar and vanilla, blending well. Carefully unroll cake; spread with cream cheese mixture and re-roll without the towel. Place on a serving plate, seam-side down; cover and chill at least 2 hours. Serves 12 to 15.

Lenise Sulin
Chapel Hill, NC

Creamy Christmas Eggnog

Garnish this holiday classic with freshly grated nutmeg...yum!

2 c. whipping cream
⅓ c. powdered sugar
1 t. rum extract
½ t. nutmeg

¼ t. allspice
1 qt. vanilla ice cream,
  softened
4 qts. eggnog, divided

Whip cream with powdered sugar, rum extract, nutmeg and allspice until stiff peaks form; set aside. In a blender, blend ice cream and 2 cups eggnog just until smooth. Pour into a large punch bowl; stir in remaining eggnog. Fold in whipped cream mixture just until fluffy. Makes about 5 quarts.

Christmas Eve Soup

The hearty flavors of potato and ham combined with carrot, celery and onion make for a flavorful and filling soup.

2 c. potatoes, peeled and diced
½ c. carrot, peeled and diced
½ c. celery, chopped
¼ c. onion, chopped
2 c. water
1½ t. salt
¼ t. pepper

1 c. cooked ham, cubed
¼ c. butter or margarine
¼ c. all-purpose flour
2 c. milk
8-oz. pkg. shredded Cheddar
  cheese

I am 11 years old and my mom and I had so much fun making recipes from one of your cookbooks. We always have this soup on Christmas Eve, and hope you will enjoy it as much as our family does.

Jessica

Combine first 7 ingredients in a large soup pot; bring to a boil over medium heat. Reduce heat; cover and simmer until vegetables are tender. Stir in ham; set aside. In a separate saucepan, melt butter; stir in flour until smooth. Gradually add milk; bring to a boil. Cook and stir 2 minutes or until thickened. Stir in cheese until melted; add to vegetable mixture and heat through. Serves 8.

Jessica Heimbaugh
Gilbert, IA

Scalloped Oyster Stuffing

Oysters are a traditional ingredient in dressings along the Southern coastal states…this dressing is sure to be the centerpiece of your holiday feast.

½ c. onion, diced
1 c. celery, thinly sliced
1 c. butter or margarine,
    softened
2 (8-oz.) cans oysters, drained
    and liquid reserved

1 c. whipping cream
¼ c. fresh parsley, chopped
½ t. salt
¼ t. pepper
3 (3½-oz.) pkgs. unsalted soda
    crackers, coarsely crushed

This will be your new favorite way to prepare stuffing!

Brittany

Sauté onion and celery in butter in a skillet over medium heat until tender. Remove from heat; stir in reserved oyster liquid, cream, parsley, salt and pepper. Set aside. Combine oysters and cracker crumbs in a large bowl; spoon onion mixture over top and toss lightly to mix. Let stand 5 minutes or until liquid is absorbed. Cover and chill until ready to use. Makes enough to fill a 16- to 18-pound turkey. Serves 5 to 7.

Brittany Thorngren
Broomfield, CO

pumpkin pretties

Fill a hollowed-out pumpkin with stuffing, veggies or salad…they look darling on a buffet table.

Stuffed Beef Tenderloin

Packed with spinach and cheese, this tenderloin will melt in your mouth!

10-oz. pkg. frozen chopped
    spinach, thawed and drained
2 t. balsamic vinegar
3 oz. Muenster cheese, shredded
¼ c. dried currants
1 egg

1 clove garlic, minced
½ t. salt
½ t. pepper
6-lb. beef tenderloin, butterflied
⅓ c. beef broth

Combine spinach, vinegar, cheese, currants, egg, garlic, salt and pepper in a large bowl; blend well. Open and flatten tenderloin; spoon spinach mixture down center of tenderloin. Bring long sides of tenderloin together, cover filling and tie with butcher's twine at one-inch intervals. Place roast in a shallow baking pan and cover with beef broth. Bake, uncovered, at 425 degrees for 10 minutes; reduce heat to 350 degrees and bake 25 more minutes for rare or 35 more minutes for medium-rare. Let tenderloin stand 15 minutes before carving. Serves 10.

Donna Dye
London, OH

Overnight Pork & Sauerkraut

Traditionally, eating pork and sauerkraut on New Year's Day will bring you good luck. Put this casserole in the oven in the wee small hours of the morning, and it'll be ready for you on New Year's Day!

2 lbs. pork loin, cut into
    1-inch cubes
2 lbs. sauerkraut, divided

2 c. sliced onion, divided
6 slices bacon, cut in half
3 c. water

Brown pork in a large skillet and set aside. Place one pound of sauerkraut in a 2-quart casserole dish. Cover with one cup onion and the browned pork. Top with remaining sauerkraut and onion. Top with bacon. Pour water over the layers and bake, uncovered, at 300 degrees overnight or for about 7 to 8 hours. Serves 4 to 6.

Pork & Raspberry Sauce

(pictured on page 8)

A tender roast pork will make your family's holiday homecoming so memorable!

3- to 4-lb. boneless pork loin roast	1 t. black pepper
	1 t. rubbed sage
1 t. salt	Raspberry Sauce

Sprinkle roast with salt, pepper and sage. Place roast on rack in shallow roasting pan. Bake at 325 degrees for 1½ to 2 hours or until meat thermometer registers 150 degrees. Cover and let sit until thermometer registers 160 degrees. Place roast on platter; serve with Raspberry Sauce. Serves 10.

Raspberry Sauce:

12-oz. pkg. frozen raspberries, thawed	½ t. nutmeg
	½ c. cornstarch
3 c. sugar	2 T. lemon juice
½ c. white vinegar	2 T. butter, melted
½ t. ground cloves	6 to 8 drops red food coloring
½ t. ground ginger	

Drain raspberries, reserving juice. Add water to juice, if necessary, to make 1½ cups. Combine one cup of the raspberry liquid with sugar, vinegar, cloves, ginger and nutmeg in a saucepan. Bring to a boil. Reduce heat; simmer uncovered 10 minutes. Blend cornstarch and remaining raspberry liquid; add to saucepan. Cook over medium heat, stirring constantly, one minute or until thickened. Stir in raspberries, lemon juice, butter and food coloring.

Robbin Chamberlain
Worthington, OH

Fresh Cranberry Ring

Serve this cranberry ring on a cut-glass plate with cool green grapes…just beautiful.

2 c. cranberries
½ t. lemon zest
¾ c. sugar
½ c. cold water
2 envs. unflavored gelatin

1 c. red wine or white
   grape juice
½ c. walnuts, chopped
2 T. lemon juice
½ c. mayonnaise

Chop cranberries in a blender or food processor; stir in lemon zest and sugar; pour into a bowl and set aside. Pour cold water in blender and sprinkle gelatin on water. Allow gelatin to soften 10 minutes. Heat wine or grape juice to almost boiling and add to blender. Blend until gelatin has dissolved. Mix cranberry mixture, walnuts, lemon juice and mayonnaise with gelatin mixture and pour into a wet 1½-quart ring mold. Refrigerate until set. Serves 8.

frosted fruit

Frosted fruit garnishes are easy. Just coat grapes or berries with pasteurized egg white and dip in super-fine sugar. You can process regular sugar in your food processor to make it extra fine. Arrange frosted fruits on a pretty, cut-glass plate around a festive spice cake.

Old-Fashioned Fruitcake

Bake this cake several weeks before you want to enjoy it, so that the flavors can blend well.

1 c. candied pineapple, chopped
1½ c. mixed candied fruit, chopped
1 c. chopped dates
2½ c. chopped pecans or walnuts
3 c. all-purpose flour, divided

1 c. butter, softened
1 c. sugar
4 eggs
¼ c. corn syrup
¼ c. orange juice
¼ c. sherry or orange juice

Combine fruits and nuts in a large bowl; coat well with one cup flour and set aside. In a large bowl, blend together butter and sugar until light and fluffy. Add eggs, one at a time, beating well after each addition; set aside. Combine corn syrup, orange juice and sherry or orange juice. Add to butter mixture, alternating with remaining flour. Fold in fruits and nuts. Pour batter into 8 greased 5"x3" mini loaf pans. Bake at 275 degrees for 60 to 70 minutes. Makes 8 mini loaves.

Rose Marie Rugger
Omaha, NE

When I wanted a fruitcake with less fruit and more nuts, I created this recipe.

Rose Marie

sweet and simple

Dress up a white frosted cake with beautiful red and green "leaves." Lightly dust a work surface with sugar and roll red and green gumdrops until flat. Use a mini leaf-shape cookie cutter to make leaves. Sweet and simple!

Hoppin' John

This traditional good-luck stew is popular in the South. Eating it on New Year's Day promises a prosperous and healthy New Year.

1 c. dried black-eyed peas
10 c. water, divided
6 slices bacon, coarsely chopped
¾ c. onion, chopped
1 stalk celery, chopped
¾ t. cayenne pepper
1½ t. salt
1 c. long-cooking rice, uncooked

Rinse peas and place in a large saucepan with 6 cups water. Bring to a boil; reduce heat and simmer 2 minutes. Remove from heat, cover and let stand one hour. Drain and rinse. In same pan, cook bacon until crisp. Drain off drippings, reserving 3 tablespoons in pan. Add peas, remaining water, onion, celery, cayenne pepper and salt. Bring to a boil, cover and reduce heat. Simmer 30 minutes. Add rice; cover and simmer 20 more minutes or until peas and rice are tender. Serves 4 to 6.

lucky year

Good luck is said to be the reward for eating black-eyed peas on New Year's Day. Try this tasty recipe to bring your family good fortune!

Tangy Corn Casserole,
page 77

casseroles galore

Planning busy weeknight meals is easy when you choose from a number of family favorites such as Cheesy Chicken Fettuccine (page 53) and Golden Chicken Divan (page 57). And when you have company coming for supper, you won't want to miss the delicious Shrimp & Feta Casserole (page 47), which will have your guests asking for seconds. You'll savor these and other delicious recipes in this chapter.

Dijon Salmon Bake

To keep fish its freshest, put it in a plastic zipping bag, seal tightly and then place inside a bowl filled with ice. Refrigerate and use within a day or two.

6-oz. pkg. baby spinach, cooked, well drained and shredded
1¾ c. cooked rice
½ t. salt, divided
¾ c. sour cream
1 egg
3 T. grated Parmesan & Romano cheese, divided

1 T. Dijon mustard
¼ t. pepper
1 lb. boneless, skinless salmon fillets, sliced ½-inch thick on the diagonal
½ t. water

Combine spinach, rice and ¼ teaspoon salt in a large bowl; set aside. Whisk together sour cream, egg, 2 tablespoons cheese, mustard, remaining salt and pepper in a small bowl. Add sour cream mixture, reserving ¼ cup, to rice mixture and stir to coat. Place in a greased 1½-quart casserole dish; top with salmon. Set aside. Add water to reserved sour cream mixture; mix well and drizzle over salmon. Top with remaining cheese. Bake at 350 degrees for 30 minutes. Let stand 5 minutes before serving. Serves 4.

Jaunae Phoenix-Bacon
Macomb, IL

family reunion fun

Don't forget nametags at your family reunion! Use a different color of tag for each family...make it easy to see which branch of the family tree each person comes from.

Southern-Style Shrimp & Rice

Surprise your family with this updated version of an old-fashioned delight.

¾ c. butter, divided
1 onion, sliced
8-oz. pkg. sliced mushrooms
¼ c. green pepper, diced
2 c. cooked long-grain and
    wild rice
1½ lbs. medium shrimp, peeled,
    deveined and cleaned

1 T. Worcestershire sauce
hot pepper sauce to taste
salt and pepper to taste
½ c. all-purpose flour
1½ c. chicken broth
½ c. white wine or chicken
    broth

In a large heavy skillet, melt ¼ cup butter over medium heat. Add onion, mushrooms and pepper; sauté 8 minutes. Add rice; toss until well blended and spread across bottom of a greased 2-quart casserole dish. Set aside. In a medium bowl, combine shrimp, sauces, salt and pepper. Arrange evenly over vegetable mixture; set aside. Melt remaining butter over medium heat in a saucepan; add flour and whisk one minute. Add broth and wine or more broth. Whisk until well blended and slightly thickened; pour evenly over shrimp. Bake at 350 degrees for 25 minutes or until bubbly. Serves 6.

Claire Bertram
Lexington, KY

substitution savvy

Broth is an easy substitution for wine in recipes. Use beef broth for red wine and chicken broth for white.

Shrimp & Feta Casserole

Chunky salsa is the secret ingredient in this savory dinner.

2 eggs
1 c. evaporated milk
1 c. plain yogurt
3-oz. pkg. crumbled feta cheese
2 c. shredded Swiss cheese
¼ c. fresh parsley, chopped
1 t. dried basil
1 t. dried oregano
4 cloves garlic, minced

8-oz. pkg. angel hair pasta,
    cooked
16-oz. jar chunky salsa
1 lb. medium shrimp, peeled,
    deveined, cleaned
    and divided
8-oz. pkg. shredded
    mozzarella cheese

In a medium bowl, combine first 9 ingredients; set aside. Spread half the pasta in a greased 13"x9" baking pan. Cover with salsa; add half the shrimp. Spread remaining pasta over shrimp; top with egg mixture. Add remaining shrimp and top with mozzarella cheese. Bake at 350 degrees for 30 minutes. Remove from oven and let stand 5 minutes before serving. Serves 6 to 8.

Jill Valentine
Jackson, TN

blender basics

Blenders are a great help in the kitchen. Use them to crush ice, purée vegetables or whip together ingredients for sauces. To clean one quickly, just add warm water and a little dish soap. Blend for a few seconds; rinse and dry.

Simple Turkey Pot Pie

Topped with buttermilk biscuits, this pot pie is surprisingly simple to prepare, yet every bit as tasty as you'd expect.

16-oz. pkg. frozen mixed vegetables, thawed and drained
2 (14¾-oz.) cans creamed corn
10¾-oz. can cream of mushroom soup
¾ c. milk
2 c. cooked turkey, chopped
2 (12-oz.) tubes refrigerated buttermilk biscuits, quartered

Mix vegetables, corn, soup, milk and turkey; pour into a greased 13"x9" baking pan. Top with biscuits; bake at 350 degrees for 35 to 40 minutes or until biscuits are golden. Serves 6.

Cathy Rutz
Andover, KS

get set for fun

Set the table with a kid's-eye view! Arrange stickers on a plastic tablecloth or cut placemats from craft paper and set out some crayons. Have kids "dress up" for dinner, wearing beads, feather boas and hats…make family dinners fun and memorable.

Turkey-Almond Casserole

This yummy dish is one of the best uses around for leftover turkey.

2 (10¾-oz.) cans cream
    of mushroom soup
½ c. mayonnaise
½ c. sour cream
2 T. onion, chopped
2 T. lemon juice
1 t. salt
½ t. pepper
5 c. cooked turkey, cubed

3 c. cooked rice
4 stalks celery, chopped
8-oz. can sliced water
    chestnuts, drained
1¼ c. sliced almonds, divided
1½ c. round buttery crackers,
    crumbled
⅓ c. butter, melted

Even my husband
likes this scrumptious
dish, and he's a real
meat & potatoes man!

Janet

Combine soup, mayonnaise, sour cream, onion, lemon juice, salt and pepper in a large bowl; mix well. Stir in turkey, rice, celery, water chestnuts and one cup almonds. Pour into a greased 13"x9" baking pan; set aside. Combine remaining almonds, cracker crumbs and butter; sprinkle over top. Bake, uncovered, at 350 degrees for 35 to 40 minutes or until bubbly and golden. Serves 6.

Janet Allen
Dalton Gardens, ID

Turkey & Wild Rice Casserole

It's easy to double or even triple this tasty recipe, and it can be made ahead and refrigerated...terrific for the holiday season when guests may drop in.

2 c. cooked turkey, diced
6-oz. pkg. long-grain and wild
    rice, cooked
10¾-oz. can cream of
    mushroom soup
6-oz. jar sliced mushrooms,
    drained
1 c. celery, thinly sliced
1 c. red pepper, chopped

We have shared this casserole with many friends over the years.

Margaret

    Combine all ingredients in a large bowl. Spread in a lightly greased 11"x7" baking pan. Cover and bake at 350 degrees for 30 to 40 minutes. Serves 4 to 6.

Margaret Scoresby
Mosinee, WI

election day supper

This casserole is perfect for serving on Election Day. Show your spirit when decorating the table for an Election Day supper...toss red-checkered fabric over tables and arrange white daisies in blue enamelware pails.

Sour Cream Noodle Bake

To roast garlic, slice off the top of the bulb, making sure to cut the tips of the cloves. Place in a square of aluminum foil, drizzle with olive oil, wrap up and bake at 450 degrees for 25 to 30 minutes. Let cool enough to handle, then squeeze the cloves out of the skin.

1 lb. ground turkey
1 t. salt
¼ t. pepper
1 bulb garlic, roasted
8-oz. can tomato sauce
1 c. cottage cheese

1 c. sour cream
1 c. shredded fontina cheese
1 bunch green onions, chopped
8-oz. pkg. medium egg noodles,
   cooked
1 c. shredded Cheddar cheese

Brown turkey in a large skillet sprayed with non-stick vegetable spray; drain. Sprinkle with salt and pepper. Stir in garlic and tomato sauce; reduce heat, simmer 5 minutes and set aside. In a medium bowl, combine cottage cheese, sour cream, fontina cheese and green onions; set aside. Spread half the turkey mixture in a lightly greased 2-quart casserole dish; top with half the noodles, then half the cheese mixture. Repeat layers. Cover and bake at 350 degrees for 30 minutes. Uncover, sprinkle with Cheddar cheese and bake 10 more minutes. Serves 6.

Tami Bowman
Marysville, OH

on the side

Serve a side of zesty herbed carrots…ready in only 15 minutes. Combine one pound of sliced carrots with ¼ cup balsamic vinaigrette dressing and cook over medium heat for 10 minutes. Top with 2 tablespoons chopped fresh parsley and 2 tablespoons chopped walnuts.

Cheesy Chicken Fettuccine

Chunks of chicken in a creamy mushroom sauce make this weeknight favorite irresistible.

10¾-oz. can cream of
    mushroom soup
8-oz. pkg. cream cheese, cubed
4-oz. can sliced mushrooms,
    drained
1 c. whipping cream
½ c. butter, softened
¼ t. garlic powder

¾ c. grated Parmesan cheese
½ c. shredded mozzarella
    cheese
2½ c. cooked chicken, cubed
8-oz. pkg. fettuccine pasta,
    cooked
Topping

Combine soup, cream cheese, mushrooms, cream, butter and garlic powder in a large saucepan over medium heat. Stir in cheeses until melted. Add chicken; heat through. Stir in pasta. Spread in a lightly greased 2-quart casserole dish; sprinkle with Topping. Cover and bake at 350 degrees for 25 minutes. Uncover and bake for 5 to 10 minutes more or until golden. Serves 8.

Topping:

⅓ c. seasoned bread crumbs
2 T. butter, melted

1 to 2 T. grated Parmesan cheese

Combine all ingredients in a small bowl.

Margaret Scoresby
Mosinee, WI

We have served this to the basketball team when they come over for dinner and also take it to church potlucks and family get-togethers.

Margaret

Crunchy Biscuit Chicken

Chicken, beans, cheese and biscuits...what more could you want?

2 c. cooked chicken, diced
10¾-oz. can cream of
   chicken soup
14½-oz. can green beans
1 c. Cheddar cheese, shredded
4-oz. can sliced mushrooms
½ c. mayonnaise-type salad
   dressing

1 t. lemon juice
10-oz. tube refrigerated flaky
   biscuits
1 to 2 T. butter, melted
¼ c. Cheddar cheese croutons,
   crushed

Combine first 7 ingredients in a medium saucepan over medium heat; cook until hot and bubbly. Pour hot chicken mixture into an ungreased 13"x9" baking pan. Separate biscuit dough into 10 biscuits. Arrange biscuits over chicken mixture. Brush each biscuit with butter; sprinkle with croutons. Bake, uncovered, at 375 degrees for 25 to 30 minutes or until deep, golden brown. Serves 4 to 6.

Mary Makulec
Rockford, IL

Swiss Chicken

This casserole can be prepared a day in advance…just refrigerate it until you're ready to bake.

4 boneless, skinless chicken
    breasts, cooked and cubed
2 c. seasoned croutons
½ c. celery, sliced
¼ c. onion, chopped
½ lb. Swiss cheese, cubed

¼ c. sliced almonds
salt and pepper to taste
2 (10¾-oz.) cans cream of
    chicken soup
½ c. mayonnaise

Place chicken in a lightly greased 13"x9" baking pan. Sprinkle with croutons, celery, onion, cheese and almonds. Add salt and pepper to taste; set aside. Combine soup and mayonnaise; mix thoroughly. Pour over chicken mixture and spread evenly. Cover and bake at 325 degrees for 50 minutes. Uncover and bake 10 more minutes. Let stand 5 to 10 minutes before serving. Serves 6 to 8.

Paula Lichiello
Forest, VA

freeze it

Need to thaw a frozen casserole? Up to 2 days before serving, set the frozen casserole in the refrigerator to slightly thaw. When ready to bake, cover loosely with aluminum foil and bake at 350 degrees for one hour. Remove aluminum foil and bake 20 to 30 more minutes or until heated through.

Golden Chicken Divan
(pictured on page 313)

This weeknight winner is quick & easy to make…it bakes in just 15 minutes!

1 lb. broccoli, chopped
1½ c. cooked chicken, cubed
10¾-oz. can cream of
    broccoli soup
⅓ c. sour cream
½ t. garlic powder

½ t. onion powder
¼ t. seasoned salt
½ c. shredded Cheddar
    cheese
1 T. butter, melted
2 T. dry bread crumbs

Cover broccoli with water in a saucepan; bring to a boil over medium heat. Cook 5 minutes or until tender; drain. In a large bowl, combine broccoli, chicken, soup, sour cream, garlic powder, onion powder and salt. Spread in a greased 8"x8" baking pan; sprinkle with cheese. Mix together melted butter and bread crumbs; sprinkle over cheese. Bake, uncovered, at 450 degrees for 15 minutes or until bubbly and golden. Serves 6.

Amy Kim
Ann Arbor, MI

This is always a favorite at church potlucks.

Amy

Chicken Tex-Mex Bake

Casseroles really taste best when they're made in advance to allow the flavors to blend. Make one the night before, then pop in the oven to bake the next day for dinner.

2 (12½-oz.) cans chicken,
    drained and shredded
2 (10-oz.) cans mild red
    enchilada sauce
10¾-oz. can cream of
    chicken soup
4½-oz. can diced green chiles
14½-oz. can diced tomatoes

2½ c. shredded Mexican-blend
    cheese, divided
1 c. sour cream
½ c. diced onion
½ t. pepper
10 flour tortillas, cut into 1-inch
    squares and divided
½ c. sliced black olives

Combine first 5 ingredients and half the cheese; mix well. Blend in sour cream, onion and pepper; set aside. Arrange half the tortillas over the bottom of a greased 13"x9" baking pan. Spoon half the chicken mixture over tortillas. Repeat layers, ending with chicken mixture on top. Sprinkle with remaining cheese; top with olives. Cover loosely with aluminum foil; bake at 350 degrees for 40 minutes or until hot and bubbly. Serves 8.

Jenny Flake
Gilbert, AZ

Simply stated...
my family loves
this dish!

Jenny

Hashbrown-Pork Chop Casserole

(pictured on page 313)

Serve a quick vegetable like steamed corn or broccoli along with these chops for a flavorful weeknight meal.

5 bone-in pork chops
1 T. oil
1 c. sour cream
10¾-oz. can cream of
   celery soup

½ c. milk
32-oz. pkg. frozen shredded
   hashbrowns, thawed
1 c. onion, chopped
1 c. shredded Cheddar cheese

In a large skillet over medium heat, brown pork chops on both sides in oil. Set aside. Combine sour cream, soup and milk in a large bowl; stir in hashbrowns and onion. Spread sour cream mixture in an ungreased 13"x9" baking pan and sprinkle with cheese. Top with pork chops. Bake, uncovered, at 375 degrees for 45 to 50 minutes or until heated through and pork chops are fully cooked. Serves 5.

Shirley Flanagan
Wooster, OH

fix it fast

Why wait for a huge pot of water to boil? Steam fresh ears of corn in just minutes. Bring 2 inches of water to a boil in a stockpot, then stand ears stem-sides down in the pot. Cover and steam until tender, about 6 to 8 minutes.

Blue-Ribbon Ham Casserole

One taste of this homemade dish and you'll see why it's a tried & true county fair blue-ribbon winner!

1½ lbs. yams, peeled, boiled
    and sliced ¾-inch thick
2 c. cooked ham, chopped
1½ c. Golden Delicious apples,
    peeled, cored and sliced

¼ t. salt
¼ t. paprika
½ c. brown sugar, packed
2 T. bourbon or apple juice
2 T. butter, sliced

Arrange half the yams in a greased 2-quart casserole dish. Layer ham over yams, then layer apples over ham. Arrange remaining yams over the apples; sprinkle with salt and paprika. Set aside. In a bowl, combine brown sugar and bourbon or apple juice; sprinkle evenly over top. Dot with butter. Cover and bake at 350 degrees for 20 minutes. Baste with pan juices; uncover and bake 25 more minutes. Baste with pan juices before serving. Serves 6.

Laura Jones
Louisville, KY

hot off the grill

When grilling vegetable kabobs to serve alongside dinner, it's easy to keep the veggies from slipping off...spear them on two skewers instead of one.

Gourmet Beef-Noodle Casserole

Cream cheese and Cheddar cheese make this casserole extra rich & creamy.

1 lb. ground beef
14½-oz. can diced tomatoes
8-oz. can tomato sauce
½ c. green pepper,
    chopped
4-oz. can sliced mushrooms,
    drained
1 clove garlic, chopped
2 t. salt
2 t. sugar
½ c. burgundy wine or
    beef broth
8-oz. pkg. cream cheese,
    softened
1 c. sour cream
⅓ c. onion, chopped
2 c. shredded Cheddar cheese,
    divided
8-oz. pkg. wide egg noodles,
    cooked

Brown ground beef in a skillet over medium-high heat; drain. Add tomatoes, sauce, green pepper, mushrooms, garlic, salt, sugar and wine or broth; cover and simmer over low heat 10 minutes. In a medium bowl, blend together cream cheese, sour cream, onion and one cup Cheddar cheese; set aside. In an ungreased 13"x9" baking pan, layer half the beef mixture, half the noodles and half the cheese mixture; repeat layers. Top with remaining Cheddar cheese. Bake, uncovered, at 350 degrees for 40 minutes. Serves 6 to 8.

Michelle Greeley
Hayes, VA

While visiting my mother, I came across this recipe she had received from a friend while they were stationed in Germany in the early 1970s. Since finding this "long-lost recipe," I've made it many times for my family.

Michelle

try this tablesetting

Small pears, apples and Jack-be-Little pumpkins make the cutest placecards. Simply hole-punch tags, slip a ribbon through each and tie to the stem.

Unstuffed Cabbage

Busy families will love this dish that's both good for you & budget friendly.

1½ lbs. ground beef
1½ t. salt
½ t. pepper
3 T. long-cooking rice, uncooked
2 t. onion, minced
2 eggs
28-oz. can diced tomatoes

6-oz. can tomato paste
½ c. brown sugar, packed
½ c. vinegar
2 t. dried onion
1 head cabbage, chopped
   and divided

Mix beef, salt, pepper, rice, minced onion and eggs together; form into 12 (one-inch) balls and set aside. In another bowl, combine tomatoes, tomato paste, sugar, vinegar and dried onion; set aside. Place half the cabbage in a lightly greased 13"x9" baking pan; top with half the tomato mixture. Top with meatballs; pour remaining tomato mixture over top. Sprinkle with remaining cabbage. Cover and bake at 325 degrees for one hour. Reduce heat to 250 degrees; bake 3 more hours. Serves 6 to 8.

Diana Krol
Nickerson, KS

tomato tip

To get richer-tasting tomato paste, pick up sun-dried tomato paste in a tube.

Deep-Dish Taco Squares

A package of taco seasoning mix and some spices ensure that this dish is full of flavor, but not too hot & spicy.

2 c. biscuit baking mix
½ c. water
1 lb. ground beef
1 green pepper, chopped
1 onion, chopped
⅛ t. garlic powder
8-oz. can tomato sauce
1¼-oz. pkg. taco seasoning mix

1 c. shredded Cheddar cheese
1 c. sour cream
⅓ c. mayonnaise-type
   salad dressing
¼ t. paprika
Garnishes: sour cream, chopped
   tomatoes, chopped lettuce,
   chopped onion

Mix biscuit baking mix and water; spread in a lightly greased 13"x9" baking pan. Bake, uncovered, at 375 degrees for 9 minutes; remove from oven and set aside. Brown ground beef, green pepper, onion and garlic powder in a large skillet; drain and stir in tomato sauce and taco seasoning mix. Spread mixture over crust. Stir together cheese, sour cream and salad dressing; spoon over beef mixture and sprinkle with paprika. Bake, uncovered, at 375 degrees 25 more minutes. Cut into squares; garnish with sour cream, tomatoes, lettuce and onion. Serves 12 to 15.

Jody Bolen
Ashland, OH

Pasta Bake Florentine

Not only is this baked pasta delicious, but the variety of vegetables makes it colorful & appealing as well.

2 T. olive oil
1 onion, finely chopped
¼ c. red pepper, chopped
½ c. mushrooms, sliced
1 lb. ground beef
½ t. salt
¼ t. garlic salt
¼ t. pepper

2 (26-oz.) jars pasta sauce
1 c. marinated artichokes,
    drained and chopped
10-oz. pkg. frozen spinach,
    thawed and drained
16-oz. pkg. rotini pasta, cooked
8-oz. pkg. shredded mozzarella
    cheese

This dish is a huge hit at our church dinner events and is always the first to go.

Jenny

Heat olive oil in a Dutch oven over medium heat. Sauté onion, red pepper and mushrooms until tender, about 5 minutes. Stir in ground beef, salt, garlic salt and pepper. Cook until beef is browned, about 5 to 7 minutes; drain. Stir in pasta sauce, artichokes and spinach until well combined. Stir in cooked pasta. Transfer to a lightly greased 13"x9" baking pan; sprinkle with cheese. Bake, uncovered, at 350 degrees for 15 to 20 minutes or until heated through and cheese is melted. Serves 8.

Jenny Flake
Gilbert, AZ

Western Hospitality Casserole

Since this recipe makes two casseroles, you can serve one and freeze the other for later, or give it away...perfect to give to a new mom or someone who's recently home from the hospital.

¾ c. all-purpose flour
2 t. salt
4 lbs. stew beef, sliced
    into 1-inch cubes
⅓ c. oil, divided
2 cloves garlic, minced
6-oz. can tomato paste
¾ c. dry red wine or beef broth

3½ c. water
1 t. dried thyme
2 bay leaves
2 (4-oz.) cans mushroom
    pieces, undrained
8-oz. pkg. bowtie pasta, cooked
12-oz. pkg. shredded
    Cheddar cheese

Combine flour and salt in a shallow dish; coat beef with mixture. Heat half the oil in a large Dutch oven over medium-high heat; brown half the meat. Set aside cooked meat; brown remaining meat in remaining oil. Set aside meat. Add garlic to Dutch oven and sauté one minute; add tomato paste, wine or broth, water, thyme, bay leaves and cooked meat. Cover and simmer over low heat 1½ hours or until meat is tender. Remove bay leaves; stir in mushrooms and cooked pasta. Divide mixture in half and pour into two lightly greased 13"x9" baking pans or two (2-quart) casserole dishes. Top with cheese and bake, uncovered, at 350 degrees for about 30 minutes. To freeze: prepare and fill casserole dish, but do not top with cheese. Let cool completely. Wrap securely with aluminum foil; place in freezer. When ready to serve, thaw at room temperature 1½ hours. Bake, covered, at 350 degrees for one hour. Uncover and top with cheese; bake 15 more minutes to melt cheese. Makes 2 casseroles (6 servings each).

Cheryl Lagler
Zionsville, PA

casserole keepsake

Carrying in a casserole? Be sure to tie on a tag with the recipe! Creative tags can be made from holiday cards or colorful scrapbooking paper.

Johnny Marzetti
(pictured on page 309)

This hearty dish brings back childhood memories of family potlucks at Grandma's house.

1½ lbs. ground beef
1.31-oz. pkg. Sloppy Joe
    seasoning mix
6-oz. can tomato paste
1¼ c. water
4 c. elbow macaroni, cooked

15¼-oz. can corn, drained
8-oz. pkg. shredded Cheddar
    cheese, divided
Optional: 4-oz. can sliced
    mushrooms, drained

Brown ground beef in a skillet over medium-high heat; drain. Stir in seasoning mix, tomato paste and water; heat and stir until blended. Spoon into a lightly greased 13"x9" baking pan; stir in macaroni, corn, one cup cheese and mushrooms, if desired. Bake, uncovered, at 350 degrees for 45 minutes. Sprinkle with remaining cheese; return to oven until cheese melts. Serves 4 to 6.

Heather Neibar
South Bend, IN

salad secret

If there's leftover salad after dinner, use it for a tasty sandwich filling the next day. Split a pita pocket, stuff it with salad, chopped chicken or turkey, sliced grapes and drizzle with salad dressing.

Shepherd's Pie

Traditionally an English dish made with lamb or mutton, this casserole has become a popular American dish typically made with ground beef.

4 to 5 potatoes, peeled
    and boiled
2 T. butter, softened
¼ to ½ c. milk
salt and pepper to taste
1 lb. ground beef
1 tomato, chopped

6 mushrooms, sliced
2 T. fresh parsley, chopped
1 T. tomato paste
¼ t. Worcestershire sauce
1 c. brown gravy
10-oz. pkg. frozen peas, thawed

This is a classic recipe everyone should have.

Tami

Mash potatoes, butter, milk, salt and pepper together; set aside. Brown beef in a skillet over medium-high heat; drain. Add tomato, mushrooms, parsley, tomato paste, Worcestershire sauce and gravy; mix well. Add peas and simmer 5 minutes; pour into an ungreased 13"x9" baking pan. Spread mashed potatoes over top; bake, uncovered, at 400 degrees for 40 minutes. Serves 4 to 6.

Tami Davidson
Santa Clarita, CA

side dish time-saver

Purchase prepared mashed potatoes at the grocery store. Heat up, blend in sour cream and cream cheese to taste, then heat up again and stir until well blended…so yummy!

Spaghetti Pie

This recipe makes three pies...make one tonight and freeze the other two to have handy for a quick family night supper.

16-oz. pkg. spaghetti, uncooked
¼ t. salt
3 eggs, divided
32-oz. jar favorite spaghetti sauce
16-oz. container ricotta cheese

2 T. Italian seasoning
1 t. garlic, chopped
16-oz. pkg. shredded mozzarella cheese
Optional: additional Italian seasoning
¾ c. grated Parmesan cheese

Cook spaghetti according to package directions, adding salt to water. Drain; place in a large bowl and cool completely. Beat 2 eggs; add to spaghetti and mix thoroughly. Divide spaghetti mixture among 3 greased 9-inch pie plates, spreading along edges to create a crust. Spoon sauce into the center of each pie plate. Mix together ricotta cheese, remaining egg, Italian seasoning and garlic; spread over sauce in each pie plate. Sprinkle each evenly with mozzarella cheese and additional Italian seasoning, if desired. Top pies evenly with Parmesan cheese. Bake, uncovered, at 350 degrees for at least 30 minutes or until cheese is melted and bubbly. To serve, slice into wedges. Makes 3 pies (6 servings each).

Wanda Baughman
Fayetteville, PA

Tamale Pot Pie

(pictured on page 310)

Not your "usual" pot pie filling...this will be a hit!

1 lb. ground beef
2 c. frozen corn, thawed
14½-oz. can diced tomatoes
2¼-oz. can sliced black olives,
    drained
1 c. plus 2 T. biscuit baking
    mix, divided

1 T. chili powder
2 t. ground cumin
½ t. salt
½ c. cornmeal
½ c. milk
2 T. chopped green chiles
1 egg

Cook ground beef in a large skillet over medium heat until browned; drain. Stir in corn, tomatoes, olives, 2 tablespoons baking mix, chili powder, cumin and salt. Bring to a boil; boil stirring frequently, one minute. Keep warm over low heat. Stir together remaining ingredients until blended. Pour beef mixture into an ungreased 9"x9" baking pan. Spread cornmeal mixture over beef mixture. Bake, uncovered, at 400 degrees for 20 to 30 minutes or until crust is golden. Serves 6.

Marian Buckley
Fontana, CA

a cool idea

An enamelware pail makes an ideal cooler for toting to the garden for summertime weeding. Filled with bottles of water or juice and ice, it keeps thirst-quenching cool drinks close at hand.

Company Baked Ziti

Layers of sour cream and two types of cheese...this pasta classic is extra rich & cheesy.

1 lb. ground beef
1 lb. sweet Italian ground
    pork sausage
1 onion, chopped
2 (26-oz.) jars spaghetti
    sauce
16-oz. pkg. ziti pasta, cooked

6-oz. pkg. sliced provolone
    cheese
1 c. sour cream
1½ c. shredded mozzarella
    cheese
½ c. grated Parmesan
    cheese

Oh-so simple to put together, yet everyone loves it!

Colleen

Brown beef, sausage and onion in a skillet over medium heat; drain. Stir in sauce; reduce heat to low and simmer 15 minutes. Layer in a greased 13"x9" baking pan as follows: half the pasta, provolone cheese, sour cream, half the sauce mixture, remaining pasta, mozzarella cheese and remaining sauce. Top with Parmesan cheese. Cover and bake at 350 degrees for 30 minutes or until hot, bubbly and cheeses are melted. Serves 6 to 8.

Colleen Leid
Narvon, PA

Three-Cheese Pasta Bake

A host of convenience products make this one of those main dishes that's super easy to whip up and everyone loves!

16-oz. pkg. frozen cheese
    ravioli or tortellini
2 T. butter
2 T. olive oil
1 red pepper, diced
1 green pepper, diced
salt and pepper to taste

26-oz. jar spaghetti sauce
8-oz. pkg. shredded
    mozzarella cheese
¼ c. shredded Asiago cheese
¼ c. grated Parmesan cheese
1 T. dried oregano

Let ravioli or tortellini thaw 15 minutes. Melt butter and oil in a large skillet over medium-high heat; sauté peppers about 5 minutes or until tender. Sprinkle with salt and pepper; set aside. Spread a thin layer of sauce in an ungreased 13"x9" baking pan. Layer half each of ravioli, pepper mixture, cheeses and oregano; pour half the remaining sauce over top. Repeat layers. Bake, uncovered, at 375 degrees for 40 to 45 minutes or until bubbly and golden. If the cheese begins to brown a little early, simply place aluminum foil over the top of the dish as it continues baking. Serves 6 to 8.

Marjorie Lischer
Longmont, CO

convenient casseroles

Tasty casserole dishes are lifesavers for a new mom. Make several and deliver them to her before the baby arrives. She can freeze them now, then simply pop dinner in the oven to bake while the baby naps.

Tangy Corn Casserole

(pictured on page 42)

Great for brunch and summertime celebrations, this side dish gets a little kick from a dab of hot sauce.

10-oz. pkg. frozen corn,
   thawed and drained
½ c. onion, chopped
½ c. green pepper, sliced
   into strips
½ c. water
1 c. yellow squash, chopped
1 tomato, chopped
1 c. shredded Cheddar
   cheese, divided

⅔ c. cornmeal
½ c. milk
2 eggs, beaten
¾ t. salt
¼ t. pepper
¼ t. hot pepper sauce
Garnishes: tomato slices and
   green pepper, sliced
   into rings

In a medium saucepan, combine corn, onion, green pepper and water. Bring to a boil; reduce heat to medium-low. Cover and simmer 5 minutes or until vegetables are crisp-tender. Do not drain. In a large mixing bowl, combine squash, tomato, ¾ cup cheese, cornmeal, milk, eggs, salt, pepper and hot pepper sauce. Add corn mixture to cornmeal mixture; stir to blend. Pour into a greased 1½-quart casserole dish. Bake, uncovered, at 350 degrees for 45 to 50 minutes or until heated through. Top with remaining cheese and, if desired, tomato slices and green pepper rings. Serves 8.

Dave Slyh
Galloway, OH

Southern-Style Spoonbread

For Southerners, this is a must-have brunch dish. Not one bite will be left.

3 c. milk
1½ c. yellow cornmeal
½ c. butter, softened

2 t. baking powder
5 eggs, separated
1 c. cooked country ham, diced

Bring milk to a slow boil in a saucepan; gradually add cornmeal, stirring constantly. Reduce heat to low and cook, stirring constantly, 10 minutes or until thickened. Remove from heat; add butter and baking powder and stir until butter is melted. Let cool and set aside. In a small bowl, use a fork to beat egg yolks until light; stir into cooled cornmeal mixture. Add ham and mix until blended; set aside. Beat egg whites at medium speed with an electric mixer until stiff peaks form; fold into cornmeal mixture until well combined. Pour into a greased 2-quart casserole dish; bake at 350 degrees for about 40 minutes or until a toothpick inserted in center comes out clean. Serves 6 to 8.

Sharon Tillman
Hampton, VA

the right size

Unsure about the capacity of a baking pan…2 quarts or one? Just measure out one quart of water and pour into the pan to check.

Fast Asparagus Casserole

The crunch of water chestnuts sets this casserole apart.

1 lb. carrots, peeled, sliced
    and cooked
15-oz. can asparagus spears,
    drained
15¼-oz. can peas, drained
8-oz. can sliced water
    chestnuts, drained
3 eggs, hard-boiled,
    peeled and sliced

⅓ c. butter, sliced
10¾-oz. can cream of
    mushroom soup
1 c. shredded Cheddar
    cheese, divided
1 c. cracker crumbs
½ t. pepper

Layer carrots, asparagus and peas in a lightly greased 13"x9" baking pan. Place water chestnuts and sliced eggs over vegetables. Dot with butter. Mix soup and ¾ cup cheese; spread over vegetable layers. Bake, uncovered, at 350 degrees for 30 minutes or until bubbly. Sprinkle with cracker crumbs, pepper and remaining cheese; bake 5 more minutes or until cheese melts. Serves 6 to 8.

Kelly Alderson
Erie, PA

when to freeze cheese

Freezing cheese causes it to turn crumbly, and while that isn't good for a recipe using fresh cheese, it's ideal in baked casserole dishes! Just thaw cheese in the refrigerator and use within a few days.

Dennis Family Broccoli Casserole

This is a family mainstay that's a cinch to make...everyone enjoys it!

2 (10-oz.) pkgs. frozen chopped
    broccoli, cooked and drained
2 T. onion, grated
6-oz. pkg. herb-flavored
    stuffing mix

½ c. butter, melted
10¾-oz. can cream of
    chicken soup
10¾-oz. can cream of
    mushroom soup

Combine broccoli, onion and stuffing mix. Place in a lightly greased 2-quart casserole dish; drizzle with melted butter. Combine soups and spoon over broccoli mixture. Do not mix. Cover and bake at 350 degrees for 30 minutes. Uncover and bake 15 more minutes. Serves 8.

Lisa Burns
Findlay, OH

Farmers' Market Casserole

Any veggies will work well...you just can't go wrong.

15-oz. can French-style
    green beans, drained
15-oz. can green peas, drained
15-oz. can whole kernel corn,
    drained
10-oz. jar pearl onions, cooked
¼ c. butter

3 T. all-purpose flour
1 c. whipping cream
½ c. shredded Cheddar cheese
salt and pepper to taste
1 t. dry mustard
¼ t. Worcestershire sauce
grated Parmesan cheese to taste

Combine vegetables in a lightly greased 13"x9" baking pan. Melt butter in a saucepan over medium heat; stir in flour. Cook together until well blended. Gradually stir in cream, stirring constantly, until sauce is thickened. Add cheese, salt, pepper, mustard and Worcestershire sauce. Stir until cheese is melted; pour over vegetables. Sprinkle with Parmesan cheese. Cover and bake at 350 degrees for 20 to 30 minutes. Serves 6 to 8.

Brad Warner
Worthington, OH

Mom's Squash Casserole

Loosely cover the casserole with aluminum foil halfway through the baking time so that the crackers don't overcook.

1½ lbs. zucchini, sliced
1½ lbs. yellow squash, sliced
1 onion, chopped
1 egg, beaten
½ t. salt

¼ t. black pepper
½ c. butter, melted and divided
2 c. round buttery crackers, crushed

Cook zucchini and squash in boiling salted water until tender, about 12 to 15 minutes; drain and mash. Add onion, egg, salt, pepper and half the melted butter. Pour mixture into a greased 13"x9" baking pan. Sprinkle with cracker crumbs; drizzle with remaining butter. Bake, uncovered, at 350 degrees for one hour. Serves 10 to 12.

Cheryl Donnelly
Arvada, CO

Many years ago, my aunt gave this recipe to my mother. She often makes it in the summer to use the bounty of squash from her garden.

Cheryl

Laura's Eggs Benedict,
page 110

breakfast
anytime

Because breakfast foods are typically easy to prepare…they are perfect to eat for just about any meal. Get your day started with Mom's Everything Waffles (page 93) or Creamy Scrambled Eggs & Chives (page 103). If you're looking for a yummy mid-afternoon snack, you'll want to try Homemade Granola (page 119). And, for a happy ending to your day, you won't want to miss Farmhouse Quiche (page 113).

Old-Fashioned Pear Preserves

You'll love this sugar & spice spread on muffins and homemade bread...pancakes and waffles, too!

6 c. pears, cored, peeled
    and sliced
1 c. water
1 T. lemon juice
1¾-oz. pkg. powdered pectin
8 c. sugar

½ c. brown sugar, packed
2 t. allspice
2 t. nutmeg
6 (½-pint) canning jars and lids,
    sterilized

Combine pears, water and lemon juice in a heavy saucepan. Bring to a boil; reduce heat, cover and simmer 10 minutes. Stir in pectin and return to a full boil. Stir in sugar; continue boiling and stirring, uncovered, one minute or until sugar dissolves. Remove from heat; stir in brown sugar and spices. Quickly fill hot sterilized jars, leaving ½-inch headspace. Wipe rims; secure with lids and rings. Process in a boiling-water bath 10 minutes; set jars on a towel to cool. Makes 6 jars.

Stephanie Mayer
Portsmouth, VA

share the goodness

Nestle a jar of Old-Fashioned Pear Preserves and a loaf of homemade bread in a basket lined with a vintage tea towel for a welcome gift.

No-Cook Strawberry Freezer Jam

Preserve the sweet taste of strawberries all year long with this easy-to-make recipe. Serve the jam over toast, waffles, or even use to make milkshakes.

7 c. strawberries, hulled
1¾-oz. pkg. powdered pectin
1¾ c. sugar, divided

1 c. light corn syrup
8 (½-pint) freezer-safe plastic
    containers, sterilized

Thoroughly crush strawberries in a large bowl; set aside. Combine pectin with ¼ cup sugar. Gradually add pectin mixture to strawberries, stirring vigorously. Let stand 30 minutes, stirring occasionally. Add corn syrup; mix well. Gradually stir in remaining sugar until dissolved. Spoon into containers, leaving ½-inch headspace; secure lids. Let stand overnight at room temperature before freezing. May be frozen up to one year. Store in refrigerator up to 4 weeks after opening. Makes 8 containers.

Dianne Gregory
Sheridan, AR

It's so simple to preserve the sunny taste of fresh strawberries!

Dianne

French Toast Croissants

Embellish this delectable morning treat with fresh strawberries and a dollop of whipped cream.

⅓ c. milk
2 eggs, beaten
1 T. frozen orange juice
    concentrate, thawed

4 croissants, halved
    lengthwise
Garnish: powdered sugar

Blend together milk, eggs and orange juice in a shallow dish. Dip croissant halves into mixture, turning to coat both sides. Place in a greased skillet over medium heat; cook until golden on both sides. Dust with powdered sugar, if desired. Serves 4.

Kathy Grashoff
Fort Wayne, IN

When summer mornings beckon with so much to do, this breakfast is quick & easy!

Kathy

Sausage Gravy & Biscuits

Enjoy these light & fluffy biscuits topped with hot sausage gravy any time of the day.

½ c. all-purpose flour
2 lbs. ground pork sausage,
    browned and drained

4 c. milk
salt and pepper to taste
Biscuits

In a medium saucepan, sprinkle flour in with sausage, stirring until flour is dissolved. Gradually stir in milk and cook over medium heat until thick and bubbly. Season with salt and pepper; serve over warm Biscuits. Serves 10 to 12.

Biscuits:

4 c. self-rising flour
2 T. sugar
3 T. baking powder

7 T. shortening
2 c. buttermilk

Sift together flour, sugar and baking powder; cut in shortening. Mix in buttermilk with a fork, just until dough is moistened. Shape dough into a ball and knead a few times on a lightly floured surface. Roll out to ¾-inch thickness and cut with a 3-inch biscuit cutter. Place biscuits on a greased baking sheet. Bake at 450 degrees for about 15 minutes or until golden. Makes 2 dozen.

Vickie
Gooseberry Patch

Pecan French Toast

This overnight, oven-baked French toast will win you raves!

1 loaf French bread, sliced
6 eggs
1½ c. milk
1½ c. half-and-half

1 t. vanilla extract
⅛ t. nutmeg
1 t. cinnamon
Sugar Topping

Arrange bread in a lightly greased 13"x9" baking pan; set aside. Beat together remaining ingredients; pour over bread. Cover; refrigerate overnight. Spread Sugar Topping over mixture; bake, uncovered, at 350 degrees for 45 to 55 minutes. Let stand 5 minutes before serving. Serves 6 to 8.

Sugar Topping:

½ c. butter, softened
2 T. maple syrup

1 c. brown sugar, packed
1 c. chopped pecans

Mix all ingredients together.

Darcie Stearns
Rock Island, IL

Buttermilk Pancakes

(pictured on page 308)

Fluffy and golden, these pancakes are just like the ones from Grandma's kitchen.

1¾ c. all-purpose flour
2 T. sugar
2 t. baking powder
1 t. baking soda
½ t. salt

2 eggs
2 c. buttermilk
¼ c. oil
½ t. vanilla extract

Combine first 5 ingredients in a large bowl; set aside. Beat together eggs, buttermilk, oil and vanilla in a mixing bowl; stir into flour mixture just until moistened. Pour batter by ¼ cupfuls onto a greased hot griddle. Turn pancakes when bubbles appear on surface; cook until golden. Serves 6.

Rita Morgan
Pueblo, CO

buttery goodness

Whip up tasty maple butter in no time...yummy on pancakes or French toast. Just combine ½ cup softened butter with ¾ cup maple syrup.

Mom's Everything Waffles

The delicious flavors of peanut butter, pecans, blueberries and even chocolate come together in this one-of-a-kind breakfast favorite...so good!

2 c. biscuit baking mix
1½ c. quick-cooking oats, uncooked
¼ c. wheat germ
½ c. chopped pecans or walnuts
2 eggs, beaten
¼ c. peanut butter
½ c. vanilla yogurt
3½ c. low-fat milk, divided
1 c. blueberries
Optional: ¼ c. mini chocolate chips
Garnishes: maple syrup, fruit topping, whipped cream

Combine baking mix, oats, wheat germ and nuts in a large bowl; set aside. In a separate bowl, whisk together eggs, peanut butter, yogurt and 3 cups milk. Add to dry ingredients and stir. Add remaining milk as needed to get the consistency of applesauce. Fold in berries and chocolate chips, if desired. Pour by ½ cupfuls onto a preheated waffle iron that has been sprayed with non-stick vegetable spray. Bake until crisp, according to manufacturer's directions. Serve with maple syrup or fruit topping and a dollop of whipped cream, if desired. Serves 4 to 6.

Tamara Ahrens
Sparta, MI

These waffles have been a Saturday morning tradition in our family since our children were very little. If a week goes by without our waffles, we try to slip them in for a weeknight meal. They have developed over time with the addition of many tasty ingredients... even chocolate chips for birthdays and Christmas!

Tamara

a sweet touch

A jar of honey is a welcome addition to the breakfast table to enjoy on hot biscuits, toast or pancakes...even drizzled in a steamy cup of hot tea. For an ideal gift, pick up flavors like orange blossom and wildflower at a farmers' market...be sure to add a wooden honey dipper, too!

Fruity Pancake Topping

(pictured on page 308)

This sweet & tangy fruit sauce will transform pancakes, waffles or yogurt into a tropical treat.

½ c. brown sugar, packed
10-oz. pkg. frozen raspberries,
    thawed

2 bananas, sliced
8-oz. can pineapple chunks,
    drained

Combine all ingredients in a blender; process until blended. Transfer to a saucepan; simmer over low heat until heated through. Makes about 3 cups.

Tori Willis
Champaign, IL

Grandma's Warm Breakfast Fruit

Keep this compote warm for brunch in a mini slow cooker.

3 cooking apples, cored,
    peeled and thickly sliced
1 orange, peeled and sectioned
¾ c. raisins
½ c. dried plums, chopped

3 c. plus 3 T. water,
    divided
½ c. sugar
½ t. cinnamon
2 T. cornstarch

Combine fruit and 3 cups water in a saucepan over medium heat. Bring to a boil; reduce heat and simmer 10 minutes. Stir in sugar and cinnamon. In a small bowl, mix together cornstarch and remaining water; stir into fruit mixture. Bring to a boil, stirring constantly; cook 2 minutes. Serve warm or cold. Serves 6 to 8.

Virginia Watson
Scranton, PA

Fresh Fruit with Creamy Sauce

You can make this dish using many different fruits depending on what's in season.

½ c. vanilla yogurt
¼ c. unsweetened applesauce
2 t. honey
1 c. apples, cored and sliced
1 c. oranges, peeled and sliced

1 c. strawberries
1 c. blueberries
1 c. raspberries
1 banana, peeled and sliced
½ c. seedless grapes

Stir together yogurt, applesauce and honey; set aside. Toss together fruit in a large bowl; divide among 6 dessert dishes. Spoon sauce over top. Serves 6.

Sonya Labbe
Santa Monica, CA

This recipe has always been in my family since I can remember.

Sonya

Winter Morning Peaches

Start your day with the aroma of warm peaches bubbling with sugar & cinnamon...scrumptious!

2 (16-oz.) cans sliced peaches
2 T. butter
⅓ c. brown sugar, packed

½ t. cinnamon
2 T. cornstarch
¼ c. cold water

Combine peaches, butter, brown sugar and cinnamon in a saucepan over medium heat. Combine cornstarch and cold water; add to peaches and cook about 4 to 5 minutes or until thickened. Serve over pancakes or waffles. Makes about 4 cups.

Cheri Emery
Quincy, IL

A scrumptious way to enjoy peaches.

Cheri

Chocolate Buttermilk Biscuits

Top these biscuits with orange marmalade or raspberry jam... either is a delicious pairing with the chocolate.

3 T. sugar, divided
⅛ t. cinnamon
2 c. all-purpose flour
⅓ c. butter

¾ c. buttermilk
½ c. semi-sweet chocolate
    chips
¼ c. butter, melted

Combine 2 tablespoons sugar and cinnamon; set aside. Combine flour and remaining sugar; cut in butter until mixture is crumbly. Add buttermilk and chocolate chips, stirring just until dry ingredients are moistened. Turn dough out onto a lightly floured surface; knead 3 to 4 times. Roll dough to ½-inch thickness; cut with a 2¼-inch round cookie or biscuit cutter. Arrange biscuits on a lightly greased baking sheet; sprinkle with sugar mixture. Bake at 425 degrees for 15 minutes or until golden. Brush with melted butter. Makes one dozen.

Kathy Grashoff
Fort Wayne, IN

clever totes

Check with your local orchard or at the farmers' market to find some wooden fruit crates and bushel baskets...they make easy work of toting breakfast fixin's from the car to the church kitchen!

French Breakfast Puffs

To make mini muffins, bake at 325 degrees for 10 to 12 minutes.

My family has always enjoyed these melt-in-your-mouth muffins.

Andrea

⅓ c. shortening
1 c. sugar, divided
1 egg, beaten
1½ c. all-purpose flour
1½ t. baking powder

½ t. salt
½ t. nutmeg
½ c. milk
1 t. cinnamon
6 T. butter, melted

Blend together shortening, ½ cup sugar and egg in a large bowl; set aside. In another large bowl, combine flour, baking powder, salt and nutmeg. Add to shortening mixture alternately with milk; stir until moistened. Fill greased muffin cups ⅔ full. Bake at 350 degrees for 20 to 25 minutes or until golden. Combine cinnamon and remaining sugar. Roll hot muffins in melted butter and then in cinnamon-sugar mixture. Makes one dozen.

Andrea Cullinan
Delaware, OH

Blueberry & Cream Cheese Strata

This berry-filled strata is just right for a breakfast with family & friends.

16-oz. loaf white bread, crusts
    removed, cubed and divided
2 c. frozen blueberries, divided
3-oz. pkg. cream cheese, cut
    into ¼-inch cubes
4 eggs

2 c. milk
⅓ c. sugar
1 t. vanilla extract
¼ t. salt
¼ t. nutmeg

Place half the bread in a greased 8"x8" baking pan; top with half the blueberries. Top with cream cheese, remaining bread and remaining blueberries; set aside. Beat eggs, milk, sugar, vanilla, salt and nutmeg at medium speed with an electric mixer until blended. Pour over bread mixture and refrigerate 20 minutes to overnight. Bake, uncovered, at 325 degrees for one hour. Serves 4 to 6.

Kathy Grashoff
Fort Wayne, IN

Orange & Walnut Brunch Cake

Don't save this delectable cake just for special occasions…enjoy it anytime!

16.3-oz. tube refrigerated
    jumbo biscuits
¼ c. walnuts, finely chopped
⅓ c. sugar
1 T. orange zest

2 T. butter, melted
½ c. powdered sugar
3 T. cream cheese, softened
2 T. orange juice

Grease a 9" round cake pan. Separate biscuit dough into 8 biscuits. Place one biscuit in center of pan. Cut remaining biscuits in half, forming 14 half-circles. Arrange pieces around center biscuit, with cut sides facing same direction. Combine walnuts, sugar and orange zest in a small bowl; mix well. Brush butter over tops of biscuits and sprinkle with walnut mixture. Bake at 375 degrees for 20 minutes or until golden. In a separate bowl, combine powdered sugar, cream cheese and enough orange juice for desired drizzling consistency. Blend until smooth; drizzle over warm cake. Cool for 10 minutes. Serve warm. Serves 6 to 8.

Jackie Smulski
Lyons, IL

cake toppers

Edible flowers are such pretty cake toppers…choose pesticide-free blooms such as pansies, violets, chamomile, lavender, nasturtiums and hollyhocks. Before using, rinse and gently shake each flower under running water, then set aside to drain and dry on paper towels.

Gorilla Bread

Like monkey bread, but better...everyone will ask for second helpings and even thirds when you serve this recipe!

½ c. sugar
1 T. cinnamon
1 c. butter
2 c. brown sugar, packed
2 (12-oz.) tubes refrigerated
    biscuits

8-oz. pkg. cream cheese, cut
    into 20 cubes
1½ c. walnuts, coarsely chopped
    and divided

Mix sugar and cinnamon; set aside. Melt butter and brown sugar in a saucepan over low heat, stirring well; set aside. Flatten biscuits; sprinkle each with ½ teaspoon sugar mixture.

Place a cheese cube in the center of each biscuit, wrapping and sealing dough around cheese. Set aside. Spray a 12-cup Bundt® pan with non-stick vegetable spray; sprinkle ½ cup nuts in the bottom of pan. Arrange half the biscuits in the pan. Sprinkle with half the sugar mixture; pour half the butter mixture over top and sprinkle with ½ cup nuts. Repeat layers with remaining biscuits, sugar mixture, butter mixture and nuts. Bake at 350 degrees for 30 minutes. Let cool 5 minutes; place a plate on top and invert. Serves 20.

Brenda Hughes
Houston, TX

Sausage & Cheddar Grits

A rich, savory version of a Southern classic…yum!

4 c. water
1 t. salt
1 c. quick-cooking grits,
    uncooked
4 eggs, beaten
1 lb. ground pork sausage,
    browned and drained

1½ c. shredded Cheddar
    cheese, divided
1 c. milk
¼ c. butter

Bring water and salt to boil in a large saucepan over medium heat. Stir in grits; cook 4 to 5 minutes. Remove from heat. Stir a small amount of hot grits mixture into eggs; stir egg mixture into saucepan. Add sausage, one cup cheese, milk and butter; blend together well. Pour into a greased 13"x9" baking pan. Sprinkle with remaining cheese. Bake, uncovered, at 350 degrees for one hour or until cheese is golden. If cheese turns golden early, cover pan with aluminum foil. Let cool about 10 minutes before serving. Serves 6 to 8.

Sharon Brown
Orange Park, FL

Grandpa's Fried Potatoes

Alongside eggs, any style, these hearty potatoes make a great country-style breakfast.

3 to 4 lbs. potatoes
1 lb. bacon
1 onion, chopped

seasoned salt to taste
salad seasoning to taste

Boil potatoes until tender; allow to cool, then peel and cube. Fry bacon and onion in a large skillet; add potatoes and seasonings. Cook until golden. Serves 6 to 8.

Michele Olds
Avon Lake, OH

Creamy Scrambled Eggs & Chives

Spoon onto buttered toast for scrambled egg sandwiches...a delicious light meal that's ready in a jiffy!

8 eggs
2 T. fresh chives, chopped
½ t. salt
¼ t. pepper

¼ c. water
2 t. butter
½ c. cream cheese, diced

Whisk eggs together with chives, salt, pepper and water; set aside. Melt butter in a skillet over medium-high heat; pour in egg mixture. As eggs begin to set, push them gently toward center with a spatula so that uncooked egg can flow toward sides of skillet. When eggs are partially set, add cream cheese. Continue cooking one more minute or until eggs are set but still moist, stirring occasionally. Serves 4.

Regina Vining
Warwick, RI

easy eggs

For the fluffiest scrambled eggs ever, try Grandma's secret...stir in a pinch of baking powder!

Smoked Gouda Grits

These smoky & creamy grits are the perfect addition to scrambled eggs and breakfast sausage...yum!

6 c. chicken broth
2 c. milk
1 t. salt
½ t. white pepper
2 c. quick-cooking grits,
    uncooked

1⅔ c. smoked Gouda cheese,
    shredded
3 T. butter, softened

Bring broth, milk, salt and pepper to a boil in a large saucepan over medium heat. Gradually whisk in grits. Reduce heat; cover and simmer, stirring occasionally, about 5 minutes or until thickened. Add cheese and butter; stir until melted. Serves 6 to 8.

Becky Woods
Ballwin, MO

breakfast in bed

Make someone feel extra special...serve them breakfast in bed! Fill a tray with breakfast goodies, the morning paper and a bright blossom tucked into a vase.

Herbed Salmon Omelets

(pictured on page 312)

To make this dish even healthier, add in some sautéed veggies like onion or green peppers…fantastic!

My husband's brother lives in Alaska, and last summer our family reunion was held there. The men went fishing all day, and the ladies tried to find new ways to prepare the fish being brought home! This recipe is delicious and couldn't be easier to make.

Carrie

¼ c. sour cream
2 T. fresh dill, chopped
2 T. fresh chives, chopped
2 T. butter, divided

¼ lb. smoked salmon, chopped and divided
6 eggs, beaten and divided

Mix together sour cream and herbs in a small bowl; set aside. Heat one tablespoon butter in a skillet over low heat. Add half the salmon; cook one minute, stirring constantly. Add half the eggs to skillet and cook, lifting edges to allow uncooked egg to flow underneath. When almost set, spoon half the sour cream mixture over half the omelet. Fold other half over and slide onto plate. Keep warm while making second omelet with remaining ingredients. Serves 2.

Carrie O'Shea
Marina Del Ray, CA

3-Cheese Western Omelet

Start the day with a ranch-style omelet baked to cheesy perfection.

¾ c. mild salsa
1 c. artichoke hearts, chopped
¼ c. grated Parmesan cheese

1 c. shredded Monterey Jack cheese
1 c. shredded Cheddar cheese
6 eggs
1 c. sour cream

Spread salsa in the bottom of a greased 10" pie plate. Sprinkle artichokes over salsa; top with cheeses. Set aside. Blend together eggs and sour cream; spread over cheeses. Bake at 350 degrees for 30 minutes or until set. Cut into wedges to serve. Serves 6.

Jane Skillin
Montclair, NJ

Ham & Cheese Bake

This is a tasty way to use any remaining ham from Sunday dinner...try Swiss or Monterey Jack in place of one of the cheeses for variety.

3 c. shredded Cheddar cheese
3 c. shredded mozzarella
   cheese
¼ c. sliced mushrooms, drained
¼ c. green onions, sliced

¼ c. butter or margarine
8-oz. pkg. cooked ham, diced
½ c. all-purpose flour
1¾ c. milk
8 eggs, beaten

This is a favorite breakfast casserole for our family.

Gloria

    Combine cheeses; sprinkle half in an ungreased 13"x9" baking pan. Set aside. In a skillet over medium heat, sauté mushrooms and onions in butter until tender; arrange over cheese. Layer ham over the top; sprinkle with remaining cheeses. Set aside. In a bowl, whisk flour, milk and eggs together; pour over cheese mixture. Bake at 350 degrees for 35 to 45 minutes; let stand 10 minutes before serving. Serves 10.

Gloria Kaufmann
Orrville, OH

breakfast bar

Wake up the family with a rise & shine omelet buffet! Set out a variety of cheeses, vegetables and meats. Everyone can layer their favorite ingredients in a mini pie plate and get just what they want.

Make-Ahead Scrambled Eggs

Start this the night before…so easy and so delicious!

3 T. butter, divided
2 doz. eggs, beaten and
    divided
½ c. milk
10¾-oz. can cream of
    mushroom soup

4-oz. can sliced mushrooms,
    drained
½ c. green pepper, chopped
½ c. onion, chopped
1 c. pasteurized process cheese
    spread, cubed

Melt half the butter in a large skillet over medium heat. Add half
the eggs; cook until lightly set. Place in a lightly greased 13"x9" baking
pan. Melt remaining butter in skillet; cook remaining eggs. Add to
eggs already in baking pan. Combine milk and soup; pour over eggs.
Top with mushrooms, pepper, onion and cheese. Refrigerate overnight.
Bake, covered, at 300 degrees for one hour. Serves 10 to 12.

Vickie
Gooseberry Patch

take a dip

Kids will love this…serve their favorite flavor of yogurt
as a yummy dip for fresh fruit!

Laura's Eggs Benedict

(pictured on page 84)

You can easily substitute split biscuits for the English muffins and even a sausage patty for the Canadian bacon...it's tasty either way.

4 English muffins, split and
    toasted
16 slices Canadian bacon
8 eggs
¼ c. plus 1 T. butter, divided
¼ c. all-purpose flour
1 t. paprika

⅛ t. nutmeg
2 c. milk
8-oz. pkg. shredded Swiss
    cheese
½ c. chicken broth
1 c. corn flake cereal, crushed

Arrange muffins split-side up in a lightly greased 13"x9" baking pan. Place 2 bacon slices on each muffin half. Fill a large skillet halfway with water; bring to just boiling. Break one egg into a dish; carefully slide into water. Repeat with 3 more eggs. Simmer, uncovered, 3 minutes or just until set. Remove eggs with a slotted spoon. Repeat with remaining eggs. Place one egg on each muffin half; set aside. In a saucepan over medium heat, melt ¼ cup butter; stir in flour, paprika and nutmeg. Add milk; cook and stir until thick and bubbly. Stir in cheese until melted; add broth. Carefully spoon sauce over eggs. Melt remaining butter; stir in cereal and sprinkle over top. Cover and refrigerate overnight. Bake, uncovered, at 375 degrees for 20 to 25 minutes or until heated through. Serves 8.

Laura Fuller
Fort Wayne, IN

Texas-Style Breakfast Casserole

Serve this crowd-pleaser on Christmas morning. If you need to keep this casserole warm while the excitement dies down, cover it with aluminum foil and put it in a 200-degree oven.

32-oz. pkg. frozen shredded
    hashbrowns
1 lb. cooked ham, diced
1½ c. shredded Cheddar
    cheese
Optional: 2 pickled jalapeños,
    chopped

8 eggs, beaten
1 c. whipping cream
½ t. garlic powder
⅛ t. nutmeg
salt and pepper to taste
1 bunch green onions, sliced

Place frozen hashbrowns in the bottom of a greased 13"x9" baking pan. Top with ham, cheese and jalapeños, if desired; set aside. In a large bowl, combine eggs, cream and seasonings; mix well. Pour egg mixture over casserole; top with onions. Bake at 350 degrees for 55 minutes. Serves 8 to 10.

Cynde Sonnier
La Porte, TX

I hosted an old-fashioned pancake supper for my husband's 40th birthday, and thinking the ladies might like something other than pancakes, I prepared this casserole. Well, the men left the pancakes for this dish and even asked for seconds!

Cynde

Eggs Olé

A short ingredient list makes this dish perfect for a quick breakfast or weeknight supper.

3 (4-oz.) cans diced green chiles
16-oz. pkg. sliced Monterey Jack
    cheese

1 doz. eggs
2 c. sour cream
salt and pepper to taste

Spoon chiles into a greased 13"x9" baking pan; top with cheese. Set aside. Beat eggs and sour cream together; pour over cheese. Sprinkle with salt and pepper; bake at 375 degrees for 30 to 40 minutes. Serves 12.

Patti Suk
Rochester, NY

Farmhouse Quiche

Salsa and sour cream make great toppings for this veggie-packed quiche.

9-inch pie crust
2 T. olive oil
½ red pepper, diced
½ green pepper, diced
2 cloves garlic, minced
¼ c. zucchini, diced
2 T. fresh basil, chopped
4 eggs, beaten

1 c. half-and-half
1 t. salt
½ t. pepper
8-oz. pkg. shredded Pepper
  Jack cheese
⅓ c. grated Parmesan
  cheese
3 plum tomatoes, sliced

Fresh tasting and packed with flavor, this is one recipe I make for our whole family all summer long.

Jo Ann

Pierce bottom and sides of pie crust with a fork. Bake at 425 degrees for 10 minutes; set aside. Heat oil in a large skillet over medium heat; sauté peppers, garlic, zucchini and basil until tender. Whisk together eggs, half-and-half, salt and pepper in a large bowl. Stir in vegetables and cheeses. Pour into pie crust and top with sliced tomatoes. Bake at 375 degrees for 45 minutes. Let stand 5 minutes before slicing. Serves 6.

Jo Ann
Gooseberry Patch

for good measure

Vintage glass measuring cups are a real find at tag sales! Look for them in rosy pink and leafy green tints as well as milk glass and jadite. Use one-cup measures to serve up cream & sugar...tuck bouquets of freshly cut flowers into oversized 4-cup measures.

Crustless Bacon-Swiss Quiche

With one less step, this quiche recipe is a real time-saver.

9 eggs, beaten
3 c. milk
1 t. dry mustard
salt and pepper to taste
9 slices white bread, crusts
   trimmed

1½ c. Swiss cheese, diced
1-lb. pkg. bacon, crisply
   cooked and crumbled

Combine eggs, milk, mustard, salt and pepper; blend well. Tear bread into small pieces; add to egg mixture along with cheese and bacon. Pour into a greased 13"x9" baking pan or 2 greased 9" glass pie plates. Cover and refrigerate 2 hours to overnight. Bake, uncovered, at 350 degrees for 45 to 50 minutes or until eggs have set. Cut into squares or wedges. Serves 12.

Sharon Monroe
Concord, NH

simple serving

No need to slice and serve...bake a quiche in muffin or custard cups for oh-so simple individual servings. When making minis, reduce the baking time by about 10 minutes, and slide a toothpick into each to check for doneness.

Oven-Baked Pepper Bacon

The ground pepper adds a spicy kick of flavor to the bacon.

1½ lbs. bacon slices

2½ t. coarsely ground pepper

Arrange bacon slices in 2 ungreased 15"x10" jelly-roll pans. Sprinkle with pepper. Bake at 400 degrees for 25 minutes, switching pans between upper and lower racks halfway through. Remove bacon when crisply cooked. Drain on paper towels. Serves 12.

John Alexander
New Britain, CT

Parmesan Breakfast Steaks

Satisfy those cool-weather appetites with this tasty breakfast main dish...serve with scrambled eggs and hashbrowns for perfection.

1 egg
1 c. Italian-seasoned dry
   bread crumbs
2 T. grated Parmesan cheese

1 lb. beef round tip steak,
   thinly sliced
1 to 2 T. oil

Whisk egg in a shallow dish; mix bread crumbs and cheese in another shallow dish. Dip steak into egg, then into crumb mixture to coat; set aside. In a skillet over medium-high heat, cook steak in oil until tender and browned on both sides. Serves 4.

Susan Biffignani
Fenton, MO

Cheddar & Bacon Breakfast Sandwiches

Substitute Monterey Jack or Swiss cheese for a variety of flavor!

3 eggs, beaten
¼ c. milk
2 T. butter
8 thick slices bread

12 slices Cheddar cheese
½ T. chopped walnuts
4 slices bacon, crisply cooked
and crumbled

In a large bowl, whisk together eggs and milk; set aside. Prepare a griddle or large skillet by melting butter over low heat. Dip only one side of 4 bread slices in egg mixture. Place 4 bread slices, coated side down, on griddle or in skillet. Top each bread slice with 3 cheese slices. Sprinkle cheese with an equal amount of walnuts and bacon. Dip only one side of the remaining 4 bread slices in egg mixture and place over walnuts and bacon, coated side up. Cook 5 minutes per side or until bread is golden and cheese is melted. Makes 4 sandwiches.

Vickie
Gooseberry Patch

Kristen's Breakfast Bake

Make this quick dish even faster to prepare by purchasing prechopped green pepper and prechopped onion in the refrigerator section of the grocery store.

2 (12-oz.) pkgs. ground
　　pork sausage
1 green pepper, chopped
1 onion, chopped
3 c. frozen diced
　　potatoes

1 c. biscuit baking mix
2 c. milk
4 eggs, beaten
8-oz. pkg. shredded Cheddar
　　cheese, divided
¼ t. pepper

Brown sausage in a large skillet over medium heat. Add green pepper and onion. Sauté just until vegetables are tender; drain. Transfer sausage mixture into a lightly greased 13"x9" baking pan. Add frozen potatoes; toss to mix. Combine biscuit mix, milk, eggs, 1½ cups cheese and pepper in a large bowl; fold into sausage mixture, mixing well. Bake, uncovered, at 400 degrees for 40 minutes or until set. Sprinkle with remaining cheese; bake for 5 to 8 more minutes or until cheese is melted and bubbly. Serves 12.

Kristen Nicholson
Norwood, MA

Brown Sugar Baked Oatmeal

Top this warm & cozy dish with seasonal fresh fruit.

½ c. butter, softened
½ c. brown sugar, packed,
   or ½ c. honey
2 eggs, beaten
3 c. long-cooking oats, uncooked
2 t. baking powder

1 t. salt
1 c. milk
Optional: chopped dried
   fruit or nuts
Garnishes: applesauce, honey,
   maple syrup

Blend together butter and brown sugar or honey. Add eggs; mix well. Stir in oats, baking powder, salt, milk and fruit or nuts, if desired. Pour into a greased 8"x8" baking pan; bake, uncovered, at 350 degrees for 30 minutes. Serve with applesauce, honey or maple syrup. Serves 4 to 6.

Sharon Demers
Dolores, CO

When I was a little girl, Mom would have freshly baked oatmeal & raisin cookies ready when I came home from school. This recipe reminds me of them.

Sharon

Homemade Granola

Enjoy this healthy favorite as a hearty, good-for-you cereal, or try it sprinkled on plain or vanilla yogurt.

2 c. quick-cooking oats,
   uncooked
2 c. whole-grain wheat
   flake cereal
¼ c. wheat germ
1 c. walnuts

1 c. sunflower seeds
1 c. raisins
1 c. flaked coconut
¼ c. butter
1 t. vanilla extract
½ c. honey

Combine first 7 ingredients; pour in an ungreased 13"x9" baking pan. Melt together remaining ingredients in a saucepan; pour over granola mixture. Bake at 350 degrees for 20 minutes, stirring after 10 minutes. Makes about 8½ cups.

Irasema Biggs
Kearny, MO

Apple & Berry Breakfast Crisp

Use sliced strawberries instead of blueberries and it's just as tasty...and a dollop of vanilla yogurt on top makes it perfect!

4 apples, cored, peeled
　　and thinly sliced
2 c. blueberries
¼ c. brown sugar, packed
¼ c. frozen orange juice
　　concentrate, thawed

2 T. all-purpose flour
1 t. cinnamon
Oat Topping
Optional: vanilla yogurt

Combine all ingredients except yogurt in a large bowl; stir until fruit is evenly coated. Spoon into a lightly greased 8"x8" baking pan. Sprinkle Oat Topping evenly over fruit. Bake at 350 degrees for 30 to 35 minutes or until apples are tender. Serve warm with yogurt, if desired. Serves 9.

Oat Topping:

1 c. quick-cooking or
　　long-cooking oats, uncooked
½ c. brown sugar, packed

⅓ c. butter, melted
2 T. all-purpose flour

Combine all ingredients; mix well.

Connie Herek
Bay City, MI

Callie Coe's Chicken
& Dumplings, page 129

weeknight
favorites

Suppertime is an important time for families on the go, and these recipes let you enjoy moments together. Try Polynesian Chicken (page 133) for a festive family night together at home. And you won't want to miss comforting favorites like Mama Ricciuti's Spaghetti Gravy (page 140) or Pot Roast & Sweet Potatoes (page 152). Bring the family back to the table with these easy & delicious choices.

Hot Chicken Salad

If you don't care for almonds, use water chestnuts for crunch!

1 c. rice, cooked
1 c. cooked chicken, diced
1 c. celery, chopped
10¾-oz. can cream of
    chicken soup
¾ c. mayonnaise

¾ c. slivered almonds
2 T. onion, chopped
1 c. corn flake cereal,
    coarsely crushed
2 T. butter, sliced

Combine first 7 ingredients in large bowl; pour into a greased 8"x8" baking dish. Top with crushed cereal; dot with butter. Bake at 350 degrees for 45 minutes. Serves 4.

Brenda Smith
Gooseberry Patch

family fun

Post a big family tree at your gathering…have everyone bring a small photo of themselves and attach to the right branch. A great way for everyone to see where they fit into the family!

Chicken Basket

Fried chicken is a wonderful picnic food and goes so nicely with coleslaw and potato salad. Easy to carry to a picnic...wrapped in layers of newspaper, this little "basket" will keep warm until you reach your destination.

½ c. all-purpose flour
1½ T. sesame seed
½ T. poppy seed
½ T. dried thyme
¾ t. dried tarragon
1 t. salt
1 t. pepper

2 egg whites, beaten
8 chicken thighs or breasts
2 T. butter
2 T. margarine
1 loaf round sourdough bread
Herb & Seed Butter Sauce

Combine flour, seeds and seasonings in a shallow bowl. Place egg whites in a separate shallow bowl. Dip chicken in egg whites; coat thoroughly with flour mixture. Melt butter and margarine in a large skillet over medium heat. Brown chicken thoroughly, about 7 minutes per side. Transfer chicken to a lightly greased 3-quart casserole dish. Bake, uncovered, at 350 degrees for 20 minutes; turn chicken over and continue to bake 20 more minutes. Remove from oven. Cut a circle in top of bread loaf; set aside. Scoop out inside of loaf, leaving a shell of about ¾-inch-thick bread. With a pastry brush, spread Herb & Seed Butter Sauce over inside of loaf and reserved top. Place chicken inside bread "basket" and set on a baking sheet. Place top of loaf alongside on baking sheet. Bake, uncovered, for 20 minutes. Remove from oven; replace top of loaf and wrap in several layers of newspaper to keep warm. Serves 4 to 6.

Herb & Seed Butter Sauce:

¼ c. butter or margarine
3 T. sesame seed
1 T. poppy seed

1 T. dried thyme
1½ t. dried tarragon

Melt butter or margarine in a small saucepan over low heat; stir in remaining ingredients.

Pat Aykers
Bayfield, CO

Fried Chicken & Milk Gravy

If you prefer, you can substitute chicken breasts, sliced in half lengthwise so they'll cook quicker.

1 c. plus ¼ c. all-purpose
    flour, divided
1¼ t. dried thyme
¾ t. onion powder
¾ t. seasoning salt
¾ t. pepper, divided

8 chicken thighs or drumsticks
⅔ c. buttermilk
2 to 4 T. oil
1 t. chicken bouillon
    granules
1½ c. milk

Combine 1 cup flour, thyme, onion powder, salt and ½ t. pepper in a large plastic zipping bag. Add chicken to bag, one or 2 pieces at a time; shake to coat well. Dip chicken into buttermilk; return to bag and shake to coat. Heat oil in a large skillet over medium heat. Add chicken and sauté 15 minutes, turning to cook evenly until golden. Reduce heat to medium-low. Cook, uncovered, 35 to 40 more minutes or until chicken is tender and juices run clear when chicken is pierced with a fork. Remove chicken to paper towels, reserving drippings; cover chicken to keep warm. Stir bouillon, remaining flour and remaining pepper into skillet drippings, scraping up any browned bits. Add milk. Cook and stir over medium heat until thickened and bubbly; cook and stir one more minute. Serve hot gravy over chicken. Serves 4.

Darrell Lawry
Kissimmee, FL

good gravy

Nobody likes lumpy gravy! If the gravy has lumps, pour it through a mesh tea strainer just before serving time.

Rosemary Chicken & Tomatoes

Enjoy tender, slow-simmered chicken with a hint of fresh rosemary.

1 T. oil
2 lbs. skinless chicken thighs
⅔ c. chicken broth
¼ c. white wine or chicken
   broth
2 cloves garlic, minced
salt and pepper to taste

6 plum tomatoes, chopped
2 green peppers, cut into strips
1½ c. sliced mushrooms
2 T. cornstarch
2 T. cold water
2 t. fresh rosemary, chopped
cooked egg noodles or rice

Heat oil in a skillet over medium heat. Sauté chicken until golden, about 5 minutes. Drain. Add broth, wine or broth, garlic, salt and pepper to skillet; bring to a boil. Reduce heat; cover and simmer about 20 minutes. Add tomatoes, green peppers and mushrooms. Simmer, covered, 15 minutes or until chicken is cooked through. Transfer chicken to a serving dish; cover to keep warm. In a small bowl, combine cornstarch, water and rosemary; stir into vegetable mixture. Cook and stir until thickened and bubbly; cook 2 more minutes. Serve chicken over noodles or rice; spoon sauce over chicken. Serves 5.

Vickie
Gooseberry Patch

Callie Coe's Chicken & Dumplings

(pictured on page 122)

This Southern favorite is the ultimate comfort food. Like biscuit dough, the less the dumpling dough is handled, the lighter and more tender it will be.

3 to 4 lbs. chicken, cut up
3 qts. water
salt and pepper to taste

4 eggs, hard-boiled, peeled
   and chopped
Dumplings

Place chicken pieces in a large pan; add water, salt and pepper. Bring to a boil; reduce heat and simmer until tender and juices run clear when chicken is pierced with a fork, about one hour. Remove chicken, reserving broth in pan. Let chicken cool; remove bones and return meat to chicken broth. Add chopped eggs. Bring broth to a boil and add Dumplings one at a time; stir well before adding each new batch of dumplings. After adding last batch, cover and simmer until tender, about 20 minutes. Remove from heat; let stand a few minutes before serving. Serves 4 to 6.

Dumplings:

4 c. self-rising flour

1 to 1¼ c. warm water

Mix flour with enough water to make a dough that can be rolled out. Divide dough into 4 batches. Roll out each batch of dough ½-inch thick on a lightly floured surface; cut into strips.

Marilyn Meyers
Orange City, FL

My grandma always made her chicken & dumplings for family reunions. She would roll out the dough with a jelly glass.

Marilyn

Gran's Rosemary Roast Chicken

Tuck some tiny new potatoes and baby carrots around the chicken for a complete meal...so simple and delicious!

4-lb. roasting chicken
1 t. salt
¼ t. pepper
1 onion, quartered

8 cloves garlic, pressed
¼ c. fresh rosemary,
    chopped
¼ c. butter, melted

Place chicken in a large greased roasting pan; sprinkle with salt and pepper. Place onion, garlic and rosemary inside chicken; brush butter over chicken. Bake, uncovered, at 400 degrees for 1½ hours, basting with pan juices, until golden and juices run clear when chicken is pierced with a fork. Serves 4 to 6.

Audrey Lett
Newark, DE

roast chicken

Is there anything more tempting than a golden-brown roast chicken? We don't think so! For the juiciest chicken, leave the skin on during roasting, even if you plan to discard it afterwards...it will hold in all the savory juices.

Polynesian Chicken

Baked chicken pieces combine with a pineapple & orange soy sauce…a delicious taste of the islands!

2 lbs. chicken, cut up
¼ c. soy sauce
1 t. ground ginger
¼ t. pepper
2 T. dried, minced onion
3 T. brown sugar, packed
8¾-oz. can pineapple chunks,
    drained and juice reserved

½ c. orange juice
2 t. cornstarch
¼ c. water
11-oz. can mandarin oranges,
    drained
4 c. cooked rice

Arrange chicken pieces in a single layer in an ungreased 13"x9" baking pan; set aside. Combine soy sauce, ginger, pepper, onion, brown sugar, reserved pineapple juice and orange juice; pour over chicken. Cover and refrigerate one hour or overnight, turning once. Bake, covered, at 350 degrees for 30 minutes or until tender. Uncover, and bake 20 to 25 more minutes or until golden and juices run clear when chicken is pierced with a fork. Remove chicken from baking pan; keep warm on a platter. Skim off fat from pan drippings. In a medium saucepan, combine cornstarch and water with pan juices; heat until thickened and bubbly. Stir in pineapple and oranges and warm through; pour over chicken. Serve with cooked rice. Serves 8.

Norma Burton
Meridian, ID

As my children have grown and started their own families, this favorite recipe is always included in the cookbooks I make for them.

Norma

Hawaii at home

Get out the tiki torches and grass skirts when serving Polynesian Chicken! Play Hawaiian music, make paper flower leis and make it a family dinner to remember.

Chicken Mozzarella

Try portobello mushrooms in this recipe...or substitute Asiago cheese for the mozzarella for a different flavor.

6 boneless, skinless chicken
　　breasts
¼ to ½ c. all-purpose flour
salt and pepper to taste
4 T. butter, divided

¼ c. white wine or chicken
　　broth
16-oz. pkg. sliced mushrooms
½ c. shredded mozzarella
　　cheese

Pound chicken breasts to about ½-inch thick. Combine flour, salt and pepper in a shallow dish. Dredge chicken in flour mixture, coating well. Melt 3 tablespoons butter in a skillet over medium heat. Add chicken; cook just until golden on both sides. Remove chicken to an ungreased 13"x9" baking pan. Add wine or broth and remaining butter to skillet; bring to a boil. Add mushrooms; reduce heat and simmer until tender. Top chicken with mushrooms; pour skillet drippings over mushrooms. Bake, uncovered, at 350 degrees for 45 minutes. Sprinkle chicken with cheese; bake 10 to 15 more minutes or until cheese is melted. Serves 6.

Mary Gildenpfennig
Harsens Island, MI

for added crunch

To get a crispy, crunchy casserole topping, don't cover the casserole dish while it's baking.

Best Friends' Greek Pasta

3 to 4 boneless, skinless
   chicken breasts
Cajun seasoning to taste
16-oz. pkg. penne pasta,
   cooked
¼ c. basil pesto sauce

2 T. garlic, minced
6-oz. jar pitted Kalamata
   olives, drained
8-oz. pkg. crumbled feta
   cheese
¾ c. Italian salad dressing

Sprinkle chicken with seasoning. Grill over medium heat until juices run clear when chicken is pierced with a fork; slice into bite-size pieces and set aside. While pasta is still hot, stir in pesto and garlic; mix well. Stir in olives, cheese and grilled chicken. Add dressing to coat; mix well. Serves 4 to 6.

Rachel Hill
Center, TX

My best friend and I went to an Italian restaurant and ordered the Greek Pasta. We loved it so much that my friend figured out how to make it. She passed this recipe on to me.

Rachel

Italian Stuffed Chicken

Don't wait for a special occasion to serve this dish. It's easy enough to whip up any night of the week…and three cheeses make it extra rich & delicious.

2 T. butter
1 c. sliced mushrooms
1 c. ricotta cheese
1 c. shredded mozzarella cheese
½ c. grated Parmesan cheese

½ c. dried parsley
¼ c. Italian-seasoned dry
   bread crumbs
4 chicken breasts
paprika to taste

Melt butter in a skillet over medium heat; sauté mushrooms until tender and set aside. In a bowl, combine cheeses, parsley and bread crumbs; mix well. Stir in mushrooms. With your fingers, separate skin from chicken breasts. Spoon mixture underneath skin; sprinkle with paprika. Arrange chicken in a lightly greased 13"x9" baking pan. Bake, uncovered, at 350 degrees for 30 minutes or until juices run clear when chicken is pierced with a fork. Serves 4.

Kathy Solka
Ishpeming, MI

Everyone will think you spent all day in the kitchen!

Kathy

Italian Chicken & Artichokes

Serve this yummy dish with a salad and garlic bread for a satisfying dinner.

This is one of the first recipes I learned to make and it's still my all-time favorite.

Nicole

8-oz. container sour cream
10¾-oz. can cream of
    chicken soup
½ c. white wine or
    chicken broth
½ c. shredded mozzarella
    cheese
½ c. grated Parmesan
    cheese
2 T. butter

2 cloves garlic, minced
4 boneless, skinless chicken
    breasts, sliced into 2-inch
    strips
14-oz. jar marinated artichoke
    hearts, drained
16-oz. pkg. rainbow rotini,
    cooked
Garnish: grated Parmesan
    cheese

Combine sour cream, soup, wine or broth and cheeses in a bowl; set aside. Melt butter in a large, heavy skillet over medium heat; sauté garlic 30 seconds. Add chicken and cook 5 to 7 minutes or until golden. Pour sour cream mixture over chicken; cover and cook over low heat 10 minutes. Add artichokes; cook 5 more minutes. Serve sauce and chicken over cooked pasta; sprinkle with Parmesan cheese, if desired. Serves 4 to 6.

Nicole Kasprzyk
Turlock, CA

Slow-Cooker Chicken with Rice

Slow cooking keeps the chicken oh-so tender and moist.

4 boneless, skinless chicken
    breasts
¼ t. salt
¼ t. pepper
¼ t. paprika
1 T. oil
14½-oz. can crushed tomatoes

1 red pepper, chopped
1 onion, chopped
1 clove garlic, minced
½ t. dried rosemary
10-oz. pkg. frozen peas
cooked rice

Sprinkle chicken with seasonings; set aside. Heat oil in a medium skillet over medium-high heat; add chicken and cook until golden on all sides. Arrange chicken in a slow cooker. In a small bowl, combine remaining ingredients except peas and rice; pour over chicken. Cover and cook on low setting 7 to 9 hours or on high setting 3 to 4 hours. One hour before serving, stir in peas. Serve over rice. Serves 4.

Vickie
Gooseberry Patch

slow-cooker secret

Don't worry about transferring slow-cooker meals into serving dishes…they'll stay nice and warm served right from the slow cooker. And if you set a hand-written table tent card alongside your slow cooker, everyone will know just what's inside.

Cheryl's Country-Style Ribs

Serve these ribs with coleslaw and corn on the cob.

7 to 8 lbs. country-style pork
    ribs, sliced into
    serving-size portions
salt to taste

2 onions, sliced
½ c. brown sugar, packed
Barbecue Sauce

A family favorite...so delicious, there are rarely any leftovers!

Cheryl

Place ribs in an ungreased large roasting pan; sprinkle lightly with salt. Top ribs with onion slices, brown sugar and 3⅓ cups Barbecue Sauce. Cover and bake at 350 degrees for 2 hours. Uncover and add remaining sauce. Increase heat to 400 degrees; bake 30 more minutes. Serves 12 to 15.

Barbecue Sauce:

2 c. catsup
1 c. water
½ c. sugar
½ c. vinegar
½ c. Worcestershire sauce

2 T. smoke-flavored cooking
    sauce
1 t. garlic powder
1 t. salt

Combine all ingredients and mix well. Keep refrigerated. Makes 4½ cups.

Cheryl Tesar
DeWitt, NE

Mama Ricciuti's Spaghetti Gravy

True Italians call it "gravy" rather than "sauce." Simmering it for several hours makes it extra flavorful.

2 T. olive oil
2-lb. pork shoulder roast
2 lbs. hot Italian ground pork
  sausage
8 cloves garlic, coarsely
  chopped
½ c. red wine or beef broth
4 (28-oz.) cans tomato sauce

18-oz. can tomato paste
4 plum tomatoes, chopped
salt and pepper to taste
2 (16-oz.) pkgs. spaghetti,
  cooked
Garnish: grated Parmesan
  cheese

Heat oil in a large saucepan over medium heat. Add pork roast, sausage and garlic. Cook until roast and sausage are browned; drain. Add wine or broth to pan; cook one minute and set aside. Combine tomato sauce and paste in a Dutch oven; stir in tomatoes. Add meat mixture, reserved wine or broth, salt and pepper. Simmer over medium heat 2 to 2½ hours. Spoon over hot pasta; garnish with Parmesan cheese, if desired. Serves 10 to 15.

Victoria McElroy
Northbrook, IL

Jen's Pulled Pork

(pictured on page 311)

Diet cola is used in this recipe because it is less sweet in flavor. There's no right or wrong amount of sauce to use…simply stir in as much as you'd like. You can also add sliced jalapeños, minced garlic or sautéed onions and green peppers.

3- to 4-lb. boneless pork loin
    roast, halved
2-ltr. bottle diet cola

2 (28-oz.) bottles honey
    barbecue sauce
8 to 10 hamburger buns, split

A recipe I created, this is now one of my most requested dishes for picnics!

Jennifer

   Place roast into a 5-quart slow cooker; add cola. Cover and cook on high setting one hour; reduce heat to low setting and cook, fat-side up, 10 to 12 more hours. Remove from slow cooker; remove and discard any fat. Discard cooking liquids; clean and wipe slow cooker with a paper towel. Shred pork and return to slow cooker; add barbecue sauce to taste. Cover and cook on low setting one more hour or until heated through. Add more sauce, if desired. Serve on buns. Serves 8 to 10.

Jennifer Inacio
Hummelstown, PA

mix & match

Whip up mix & match napkin rings from ribbon scraps… so simple. For each ring, fold a 6-inch length of ribbon in half, right sides facing, and sew ends together with a ¼-inch seam allowance. Turn the rings right side out, and slip them around rolled napkins.

Pork Loin & Potatoes

You can substitute rib chops for the pork loin.

1 T. olive oil
1 T. butter
4½-inch-thick pork loin
4 potatoes, peeled and
    cut into ¼-inch lengths
1 medium onion, sliced
½ t. salt

⅛ t. pepper
2 t. lemon juice
1 t. dried oregano
1 green pepper, quartered
Garnish: 1 tomato, cut into
    wedges

Heat oil and butter in a 10-inch skillet over medium heat. Brown pork loin on all sides. Arrange potatoes and onion in skillet; sprinkle with salt and next 3 ingredients. Cook over low heat 30 minutes, stirring occasionally. Add green pepper; cook 5 minutes. Garnish, if desired. Serves 4.

Patricia Murdick
Three Rivers, MI

Pork Chops with Apple Stuffing

This makes a warm & cozy meal to share with friends.

1 T. olive oil
3 T. butter, divided
5 boneless pork chops
1 apple, cored and chopped

½ c. onion, chopped
1⅔ c. water
6-oz. pkg. stuffing mix

Heat oil and one tablespoon butter in a large skillet over medium heat. Add pork chops; cook 8 to 10 minutes, turning once. Remove chops; cover to keep warm. Melt remaining butter in skillet; add apple and onion. Cook 3 to 5 minutes, stirring occasionally, until tender. Add water; bring to a boil. Stir in stuffing mix; remove from heat. Arrange chops over stuffing mixture; cover and let stand 5 minutes before serving. Serves 5.

Sherry Noble
Kennett, MO

Pot o' Gold Pork Chops

A mixture of sour cream, bacon, pimento and pepper make a yummy sauce for this tasty dish.

4 pork chops
salt and pepper to taste
1 T. oil
2 T. onion, chopped
2 T. butter
1 t. salt
2 T. all-purpose flour

1 c. sour cream
2 (15¼-oz.) cans corn, drained
½ lb. bacon, crisply cooked and
   crumbled
2 T. green pepper, chopped
1 T. pimento, chopped

This all-time family favorite recipe was passed on to me by my mother-in-law.

Kim

Sprinkle pork chops with salt and pepper. Heat oil in a skillet; brown chops on both sides. Remove from skillet; set aside. Sauté onion in butter until translucent; blend in salt and flour. Stir in sour cream until smooth; add corn, bacon, green pepper and pimento. Spoon into a greased 13"x9" baking pan; top with pork chops. Bake, uncovered, at 350 degrees for 45 minutes. Serves 4.

Kim Hood
Beaumont, TX

Sweet & Sauerkraut Brats

Perfect for tailgaiting or a fall supper, these sandwiches go nicely with chips, fries or potato salad.

1½ to 2 lbs. bratwurst, cut into
    bite-size pieces
27-oz. can sauerkraut
4 tart apples, cored, peeled
    and chopped

¼ c. onion, chopped
¼ c. brown sugar, packed
1 t. caraway seed
4 to 6 hard rolls, split
Garnish: spicy mustard

Place bratwurst in a 5- to 6-quart slow cooker. Toss together sauerkraut, apples, onion, brown sugar and caraway seed; spoon over bratwurst. Cover and cook on high setting 1 hour; reduce heat to low setting and cook 2 to 3 more hours, stirring occasionally. Fill rolls, using a slotted spoon. Serve with mustard on the side, if desired. Serves 4 to 6.

Jo Ann
Gooseberry Patch

I like to pop this into the slow cooker on Saturday mornings. Later, when I get home from a day of barn sale-ing with friends, I know a hearty meal will be ready to serve my family!

Jo Ann

picnic perfect

Keep picnics festive and comfy...bring along colorful, soft quilts and blankets for lunch in the shade. Once lunch is over, those soft and cozy quilts also create a perfect spot for napping!

Beef & Broccoli Wellington

(pictured on page 308)

Ground beef makes this a quick take on an old classic...yummy!

1½ lbs. ground beef
1 onion, chopped
6½-oz. can mushroom stems
    and pieces, drained
20-oz. pkg. frozen chopped
    broccoli, thawed

2 (8-oz.) pkgs. shredded
    mozzarella cheese
8-oz. container sour cream
2 (8-oz.) tubes refrigerated
    crescent rolls

Brown ground beef with onion and mushrooms in a skillet over medium heat; drain. Stir in broccoli and cheese. When cheese is melted, stir in sour cream. Line a lightly greased 13"x9" pan with one tube crescent rolls. Spoon ground beef mixture over rolls; arrange remaining of tube rolls on top. Bake, uncovered, at 350 degrees for 15 minutes or until golden. Cut into squares to serve. Serves 6.

Cindy Kerekes
Wharton, NJ

Chili Crescent Cheese Dogs

(pictured on page 314)

So easy to make, the kids will love to help out!

8-oz. tube refrigerated
    crescent rolls
8 hot dogs

1 c. shredded Cheddar cheese
1 c. chili

Separate crescent rolls into triangles. Place one hot dog in middle of each dough triangle; sprinkle each with cheese. Spoon chili over cheese. Fold dough corners inward to partially cover each hot dog, pressing ends to seal. Arrange on an ungreased baking sheet. Bake at 425 degrees for 10 to 12 minutes or until crescents are golden and hot dogs are heated through. Serves 8.

Jen Martineau
Delaware, OH

Ted's Favorite Meatballs

These are delicious…great served over buttered noodles. Very different from your average meatball!

2 lbs. ground beef
1½ c. soft bread crumbs
1½-oz. pkg. dry onion
    soup mix
8-oz. container sour cream
1 egg, beaten

⅓ c. all-purpose flour
1 t. paprika
¼ c. butter
10¾-oz. can cream of
    chicken soup
¾ c. milk

Combine ground beef, crumbs, soup mix, sour cream and egg in a large bowl; form into walnut-size meatballs. Combine flour and paprika; roll meatballs in flour mixture. Melt butter in a large skillet over medium-high heat. Brown meatballs; drain. Blend soup and milk and pour over browned meatballs. Cover and simmer about 20 minutes. Serves 6 to 8.

Susie Backus
Gooseberry Patch

make it quick

Making lots of mini meatballs? Grab a melon baller and start scooping…you'll be done in record time!

Mexican Burgers

Chili powder, cumin and Pepper Jack cheese add a little zip to these tasty burgers.

1 avocado, pitted, peeled and
    diced
1 plum tomato, diced
2 green onions, chopped
1 to 2 t. lime juice
1¼ lbs. ground beef
1 egg, beaten
¾ c. to 1 c. nacho-flavored
    tortilla chips, crushed

¼ c. fresh cilantro,
    chopped
½ t. chili powder
½ t. ground cumin
salt and pepper to taste
1¼ c. shredded Pepper Jack
    cheese
5 hamburger buns, split

Mix together avocado, tomato, onions and lime juice; mash slightly and set aside. Combine ground beef, egg, chips and seasonings in a large bowl. Form into 5 patties; grill over medium-high heat to desired doneness, turning to cook on both sides. Sprinkle cheese over burgers; grill until melted. Serve on buns; spread with avocado mixture. Serves 5.

Stacie Avner
Delaware, OH

One night our large family all wanted burgers, but disagreed on the type of burgers we wanted. So we made traditional cheeseburgers and these Mexican Burgers. When dinner was done, even the kids agreed these beat the cheeseburgers.

Stacie

good to go

It's a good idea to keep aluminum foil, plastic zipping bags and plastic wrap on hand for wrapping up leftovers, or for someone who may just want to take a sampler plate home!

Cheesy Beef & Bacon Burger Meatloaf

Minimal prep & maximum flavor make this recipe perfect for busy weeknights or casual get-togethers.

1 lb. bacon, crisply cooked, crumbled and divided
1½ lbs. ground beef sirloin
1½ c. shredded Cheddar cheese
2 eggs, beaten
⅓ c. dry bread crumbs

⅓ c. mayonnaise
1 T. Worcestershire sauce
½ t. salt
½ t. pepper
½ c. catsup
¼ t. hot pepper sauce
3 T. Dijon mustard

Set aside ½ cup bacon for topping. Combine remaining bacon, ground beef, cheese, eggs, crumbs, mayonnaise, Worcestershire sauce, salt and pepper in a large bowl; set aside. Mix together catsup, hot sauce and mustard; set aside 3 tablespoons of mixture. Add remaining catsup mixture to beef mixture; blend well. Press into an ungreased 9"x5" loaf pan; spread reserved catsup mixture over top and sprinkle with reserved bacon. Bake, uncovered, at 350 degrees for 50 to 60 minutes or until done. Remove from oven; let stand 5 to 10 minutes before slicing. Serves 6 to 8.

Kelly Masten
Hudson, NY

Growing up in a large family, we ate a lot of meatloaf. This recipe always kept us coming back for more!

Kelly

Pot Roast & Sweet Potatoes

(pictured on page 315)

The sweet potatoes have such a good flavor in this recipe.

1½- to 2-lb. boneless beef
    chuck roast
2 T. oil
1 onion, thinly sliced
3 sweet potatoes, peeled
    and quartered
⅔ c. beef broth

¾ t. celery salt
¼ t. salt
¼ t. pepper
¼ t. cinnamon
1 T. cornstarch
2 T. cold water

In a skillet, brown roast on all sides in hot oil; drain. Place onion and sweet potatoes in slow cooker; top with roast. Combine broth and seasonings; pour over all. Cover and cook on low setting 7 to 8 hours or on high settings 4 to 5 hours.

Place roast on a serving platter, surrounded with vegetables; keep warm. Combine cornstarch and water in a small saucepan; add one cup of juices from slow cooker. Cook and stir over medium heat until thickened and bubbly; continue cooking and stirring 2 more minutes. Serve gravy with roast. Serves 4.

Barbara Scmeckpeper
Minoka, IL

Pronto Pasta Skillet

You can cook the pasta and chop the veggies ahead of time to make it even quicker.

1 lb. boneless beef sirloin steak, sliced into thin strips
¼ c. balsamic vinaigrette, divided
14½-oz. can stewed tomatoes, undrained
1 onion, sliced
1 green pepper, chopped
8-oz. can sliced mushrooms, drained
½ c. pasteurized process cheese sauce
16-oz. pkg. penne pasta, cooked

In a large skillet over medium-high heat, brown steak in 2 tablespoons vinaigrette 2 minutes or until browned on all sides. Stir in tomatoes, onion, green pepper, mushrooms and remaining vinaigrette. Bring to a boil; reduce heat to medium and simmer 10 minutes or until onion and pepper are crisp-tender. Remove from heat. Spoon cheese sauce over top. Let stand 2 to 3 minutes or until cheese is melted. Serve over cooked pasta. Serves 4.

Kathy Epperly
Wichita, KS

I like to whip this up right after church since it's both quick & easy.

Kathy

Philly Cheesesteak Sandwiches

Onion, garlic, mushrooms and green pepper spooned over layers of beef and topped with melted cheese makes for a hearty meal-on-a-bun.

2 T. butter
1 lb. beef top or ribeye steak,
    thinly sliced
seasoned salt and pepper
    to taste
1 onion, sliced

1 clove garlic, minced
Optional: 1 c. sliced mushrooms
1 green pepper, thinly sliced
1 lb. provolone, Gouda or Swiss
    cheese, sliced
6 hoagie buns or baguettes, split

Melt butter in a skillet over medium heat until slightly browned. Add steak; sprinkle with seasoned salt and pepper and sauté just until browned. Add onion, garlic, mushrooms, if desired, and green pepper; stir. Cover and simmer 5 to 7 minutes or until onion and pepper are tender. Add additional salt and pepper to taste. Remove from heat; set aside. Place 2 to 3 cheese slices in each bun; top each with 2 to 3 tablespoonfuls of steak mixture. Top with additional cheese, if desired. Wrap each sandwich in aluminum foil; bake at 350 degrees for 10 to 15 minutes or until cheese is melted. Makes 6 sandwiches.

Amy Michalik
Norwalk, IA

flavorful fries

For zesty French fries that are anything but boring, spray frozen fries with non-stick olive oil spray and sprinkle with your favorite spice blend like Italian, Cajun or steakhouse seasoning. Spread on a baking sheet and bake as directed...wow!

Better-than-Ever Beef Stroganoff

You only need one skillet to whip up this favorite.

1½ lbs. round steak, sliced
¼ c. all-purpose flour
pepper to taste
½ c. butter
4-oz. can sliced mushrooms,
    drained
½ c. onion, chopped

1 clove garlic, minced
10½-oz. can beef broth
10¾-oz. can cream of
    mushroom soup
1 c. sour cream
6-oz. pkg. medium egg
    noodles, cooked

Dredge steak in flour; sprinkle with pepper. Melt butter in a skillet over medium heat. Add steak and brown on both sides. Add mushrooms, onion and garlic; sauté until tender. Stir in broth and reduce heat; cover and simmer one hour. Blend in soup and sour cream; simmer 5 more minutes. Do not boil. Spoon over warm noodles to serve. Serves 4.

Trisha MacQueen
Bakersfield, CA

Garlic & Swiss Steak

Just like Grandma used to make…serve with baked potatoes.

⅓ c. all-purpose flour
1 t. salt
½ t. pepper
1½ lbs. beef round steak, cut
    into serving-size portions

2 T. oil
14-oz. can stewed tomatoes
½ c. onion, chopped
½ green pepper, chopped
2 cloves garlic, minced

Combine flour, salt and pepper; sprinkle over steak and pound into both sides. In a large skillet, brown steak in oil over medium heat; transfer to a lightly greased 13"x9" baking pan. Combine remaining ingredients; pour over steak. Cover and bake at 350 degrees for one to 1½ hours or until tender. Serves 6.

Jacqueline Kurtz
Reading, PA

Baked Steak with Gravy

Serve this dish with mashed potatoes for a perfect pairing.

1 c. all-purpose flour
⅛ t. salt
⅛ t. pepper
6 to 8 beef cube steaks
1 t. butter

2 (10¾-oz.) cans cream of
    mushroom soup
2½ c. water
Optional: 4-oz. can sliced
    mushrooms, drained

Mix flour, salt and pepper in a shallow bowl. Dredge meat in flour mixture. Melt butter in a skillet over medium heat; add meat and brown on both sides. Arrange meat in a lightly greased 13"x 9" baking pan; set aside. In a bowl, combine soup, water and mushrooms, if desired. Pour soup mixture over meat; cover and bake at 325 degrees for 45 to 50 minutes. Uncover; bake 15 more minutes. Serves 6 to 8.

Amy Halstead
Winfield, WV

As a wedding present, a dear friend hand-copied 75 of her "tried & true" recipes...this is one. Every time I make one of her special dishes, I smile and think loving thoughts of Miss Nancy.

Amy

Flaky Beef Turnovers

Be sure to cut the potatoes in very small pieces so they'll be done by the time the pastry shells are golden.

6-oz. boneless ribeye steak,
    cut into large pieces
1 potato, peeled and diced
3 T. dry onion soup mix
2 T. catsup

1 t. Worcestershire sauce
1 T. fresh parsley, chopped
10-oz. pkg. puff pastry
    shells, thawed

Combine steak, potatoes, soup mix, catsup, Worcestershire sauce and parsley in a large bowl. On a lightly floured surface, roll out each pastry shell into a 7-inch circle. Fill each pastry circle with approximately ¼ cup meat mixture, then lightly brush pastry edges with water. Fold circles in half and seal edges with tines of a fork. Cut several slits in the top of each turnover to vent the steam; place on a lightly greased baking sheet. Bake at 400 degrees for 20 to 25 minutes or until golden. Makes 6 turnovers.

Kay Marone
Des Moines, IA

My family loves it when I bake this dish...it's so tasty!

Kay

Herbed Shrimp Tacos

These tacos are great to make in the summer...simply grill the shrimp on metal skewers after marinating. They're so good!

juice of 1 lime
½ c. plus 1 T. fresh cilantro,
    chopped and divided
½ t. salt
½ t. pepper
⅛ t. dried thyme
⅛ t. dried oregano
1 lb. uncooked medium shrimp,
    peeled and cleaned

½ c. radishes, shredded
½ c. green cabbage, shredded
½ c. red onion, chopped
Optional: 2 T. oil
10 (6-inch) flour tortillas,
    warmed
Garnish: guacamole

Combine lime juice, one tablespoon cilantro, salt, pepper and herbs in a large plastic zipping bag; mix well. Add shrimp; close bag and refrigerate at least 1 hour. Mix together radishes, cabbage, onion and remaining cilantro; set aside. Thread shrimp onto skewers; grill over medium-high heat until pink and cooked through or heat oil in a skillet over medium heat and sauté shrimp until done. Spoon into warm tortillas; garnish with guacamole and cabbage mixture. Serves 10.

Lori Vincent
Alpine, UT

Eggplant Parmesan

This is a down-home dish that's great to enjoy with family & friends no matter what the occasion. Serve it atop spaghetti noodles.

2 eggs, beaten
1 T. water
2 eggplants, peeled and
    sliced ¼-inch thick
2 c. Italian-flavored dry bread
    crumbs

1½ c. grated Parmesan cheese,
    divided
27¾-oz. jar garden-style pasta
    sauce, divided
1½ c. shredded mozzarella
    cheese

Combine eggs and water in a shallow bowl. Dip eggplant slices into egg mixture. Arrange slices in a single layer on a greased baking sheet; bake at 350 degrees for 25 minutes or until golden. Set aside. Mix bread crumbs and ½ cup Parmesan cheese; set aside. Spread a small amount of sauce in an ungreased 13"x9" baking pan; layer half the eggplant, one cup sauce and one cup crumb mixture. Repeat layers. Cover and bake for 45 minutes. Uncover; sprinkle with mozzarella cheese and remaining Parmesan cheese. Bake, uncovered, 10 more minutes. Cut into squares. Serves 6 to 8.

Tammy Dillow
Raceland, KY

crumbs in an instant

Homemade bread crumbs are a snap! Just place Italian bread cubes in a food processor and pulse until the texture becomes fine.

Santa Fe Grilled Veggie Pizzas

Make sure to cut the vegetables into equal-size pieces so that they will grill evenly.

10-oz. tube refrigerated pizza
    dough
1 lb. portabella mushrooms,
    stems removed
1 red pepper, quartered
1 yellow pepper, quartered
1 zucchini, cut lengthwise
    into ½-inch-thick slices

1 yellow squash, cut
    lengthwise into ½-inch-
    thick slices
¾ t. salt
1 c. Alfredo sauce
1¼ c. smoked mozzarella
    cheese, shredded

Lightly dust 2 baking sheets with flour. On a lightly floured surface, press dough into a 15"x11" rectangle. Cut into quarters; place 2 on each baking sheet. Lightly coat vegetables with non-stick vegetable spray; sprinkle with salt. Grill vegetables over medium-high heat until tender, about 10 minutes. Cut mushrooms and peppers into slices. Cut squash in half crosswise. Grill 2 pieces pizza dough at a time one minute or until golden. With tongs, turn dough over and grill 30 more seconds or until firm. Return to baking sheets. Spread sauce over crusts; top with vegetables and cheese. Grill pizzas, covered, 2 to 3 more minutes or until cheese melts. Serves 4.

April Jacobs
Loveland, CO

While waiting for a train in Santa Fe, we stopped for lunch at a little restaurant and ordered grilled vegetable pizza. It was so tasty, I had to find a way to recreate it when we returned home to our ranch in Colorado!

April

grill tricks

When grilling veggies, baste them with a simple marinade that's big on flavor. Whisk together ½ cup melted butter, ½ cup lemon juice and one tablespoon freshly chopped basil.

Curried Harvest
Bisque, page 193

comforting soups & stews

Soups & stews are the ultimate in comfort food. Nothing soothes the soul more than a hearty bowl of Savory Vegetable Soup (page 169). Your whole family will love Cheesy Wild Rice Soup (page 175). And for one of those cold winter nights, invite friends over for some One-Pot Spicy Black Bean Chili (page 185).

Broccoli-Cheddar Soup

Frozen broccoli makes this soup super quick to whip up, but you can substitute fresh broccoli if you have some on hand.

1½ c. water
10-oz. pkg. frozen broccoli, thawed
2 T. butter
1 cube chicken bouillon
2 T. dried, minced onion
2¼ c. milk, divided
10¾-oz. can Cheddar cheese soup

1 c. shredded Cheddar cheese
½ t. Worcestershire sauce
⅛ t. salt
⅛ t. pepper
⅛ t. garlic salt
2 T. all-purpose flour

Combine water, broccoli, butter, bouillon cube and onion in a large Dutch oven; cook over medium heat until onion is tender. Add 2 cups milk, soup, cheese, Worcestershire sauce, salt, pepper and garlic salt; cook over low heat until cheese melts. Stir in flour and remaining milk; heat until thickened. Serves 4.

Lisa Peterson
Sabina, OH

Baked Potato Soup

You'll love this hearty soup with all the flavors of our favorite baked potato toppings...scrumptious!

3 lbs. redskin potatoes, cubed
¼ c. butter or margarine
¼ c. all-purpose flour
2 qts. half-and-half
16-oz. pkg. pasteurized process cheese spread, melted

1 t. hot pepper sauce
white pepper and garlic powder to taste
Garnishes: cooked and crumbled bacon, shredded Cheddar cheese, snipped fresh chives

Cover potatoes with water in a large saucepan; bring to a boil. Boil 10 minutes or until potatoes are almost tender; drain and set aside. Melt butter in a large Dutch oven over low heat; add flour, mixing until smooth. Gradually add half-and-half, stirring constantly. Continue to stir until smooth and begins to thicken. Add melted cheese; stir well. Add potatoes, hot pepper sauce and seasonings. Cover and simmer over low heat 30 minutes. Sprinkle with garnishes as desired. Serves 8.

Linda Stone
Cookeville, TN

Savory Vegetable Soup

Chock-full of vegetables, cheese and beef...this soup will quickly become a part of your recipe file.

¾ c. onion, chopped
¾ c. carrots, shredded
¾ c. celery, diced
1 t. dried basil
3 T. butter
¼ c. all-purpose flour
3 c. chicken broth

4 c. potatoes, peeled and cubed
1 lb. ground beef, browned
8-oz. pkg. pasteurized process
    cheese spread, cubed
1½ c. milk
salt and pepper to taste
¼ c. sour cream

In a large saucepan over medium heat, sauté onion, carrots, celery and basil in butter 5 minutes; stir in flour, broth, potatoes and beef. Cover; simmer 15 minutes or until potatoes are tender. Add cheese, milk, salt and pepper; cook until cheese is melted. Remove from heat and blend in sour cream. Serves 4 to 6.

Natasha Roe
Sebring, FL

Rainy-Day Tomato Soup

Topped with buttery fresh-baked croutons, here is a tomato soup that is anything but ordinary.

2 T. olive oil
1 onion, thinly sliced
3 to 4 T. garlic, chopped
1 c. celery, chopped
½ c. carrot, peeled and cut into
    2-inch sticks

28-oz. can crushed
    tomatoes
2½ c. vegetable broth
2 t. dried basil
1 t. dried thyme
Italian Croutons

Heat oil in a Dutch oven over medium heat; add onion and garlic and sauté until onion is translucent. Add celery and carrot; cook 5 more minutes. Add remaining ingredients and bring to a boil. Reduce heat; cover and simmer 1½ hours or until thickened. Ladle soup into 4 bowls; top each serving evenly with Italian Croutons. Serves 4.

Italian Croutons:

1 loaf day-old bread, crusts
    removed

½ c. butter, melted
1 T. Italian seasoning

Cube bread and place in a large plastic zipping bag; set aside. Combine butter and seasoning; pour over bread. Mix well; arrange bread cubes on an ungreased baking sheet. Bake at 425 degrees for 10 minutes; turn bread cubes and bake 5 more minutes.

Rosie Sabo
Toledo, OH

best basil

Nothing perks up the flavor of tomato soup like fresh basil! Keep a pot of basil on the kitchen windowsill and just snip off a few leaves whenever you need some.

Tomato-Ravioli Soup

This soup has a light, smooth flavor...there's always an empty pot after dinner!

1 lb. ground beef
28-oz. can crushed tomatoes
6-oz. can tomato paste
2 c. water
1½ c. onion, chopped
2 cloves garlic, minced
¼ c. fresh parsley, chopped
¾ t. dried basil

½ t. dried oregano
¼ t. dried thyme
½ t. onion salt
½ t. salt
¼ t. pepper
½ t. sugar
9-oz. pkg. frozen cheese ravioli
¼ c. grated Parmesan cheese

In a Dutch oven, brown beef over medium heat; drain. Stir in tomatoes, tomato paste, water, onion, garlic and seasonings. Bring to a boil. Reduce heat; cover and simmer 30 minutes. Cook ravioli according to package directions; drain. Add ravioli to soup and heat through. Stir in Parmesan cheese; serve immediately. Serves 6 to 8.

Heather Quinn
Gilmer, TX

Curried Pumpkin Soup

This soup freezes well...just add the cream after thawing.

16-oz. pkg. sliced mushrooms
½ c. onion, chopped
2 T. butter
2 T. all-purpose flour
1 T. curry powder
3 c. chicken or vegetable broth
15-oz. can pumpkin

1 T. honey
⅛ t. nutmeg
salt and pepper to taste
1 c. whipping cream or
    evaporated milk
Garnishes: sour cream,
    croutons

Sauté mushrooms and onion in butter in a large saucepan over medium heat until softened. Add flour and curry powder; cook 5 minutes, stirring constantly. Add broth, pumpkin, honey, nutmeg, salt and pepper. Reduce heat and simmer 15 minutes, stirring occasionally. Stir in cream or milk; heat through without boiling. Garnish servings with a dollop of sour cream and croutons, if desired. Serves 6.

Carol Allston-Stiles
Newark, DE

North Woods Bean Soup

Here is a hearty soup to come home to on a brisk, cool evening.

½ lb. turkey Kielbasa, halved
    lengthwise and sliced
    ½-inch thick
1 c. baby carrots, chopped
1 c. onion, chopped
2 cloves garlic, minced

4 c. chicken broth
½ t. Italian seasoning
½ t. pepper
2 (15.8-oz.) cans Great Northern
    beans, drained and rinsed
6-oz. pkg. baby spinach

Spray a Dutch oven with non-stick vegetable spray; heat over medium-high heat. Add turkey, carrots, onion and garlic; sauté 3 minutes, stirring occasionally. Reduce heat to medium; cook 5 minutes. Add broth, seasonings and beans. Bring to a boil; reduce heat and simmer 5 minutes. Place 2 cups of soup in a blender or food processor. Process until smooth; return processed soup to pan. Simmer 5 more minutes; remove from heat. Add spinach, stirring until it wilts. Serves 5.

Sharon Demers
Dolores, CO

Cheesy Wild Rice Soup

Garnish each bowl of this soup with a little extra crispy bacon...yummy!

9 to 10 slices bacon, diced
1 onion, chopped
2 (10¾-oz.) cans cream of
   potato soup
1½ c. cooked wild rice
2 pts. half-and-half
2 c. American cheese, shredded
Optional: Biscuit Bowls

In a skillet over medium heat, sauté bacon and onion together until bacon is crisp and onion is tender. Drain and set aside. Combine soup and rice in a medium saucepan; stir in bacon mixture, half-and-half and cheese. Cook over low heat until cheese melts, stirring occasionally. Serve in Biscuit Bowls, if desired. Serves 6 to 8.

Tanya Graham
Lawrenceville, GA

Biscuit Bowls:

Homemade soup is even more special when served in a fresh-baked biscuit bowl.

16.3-oz. tube refrigerated
   jumbo flaky biscuits
non-stick vegetable spray

Flatten each biscuit into a 5-inch round. Invert 8 (6-ounce) custard cups, several inches apart, on a lightly greased baking sheet. Spray bottoms of cups with non-stick vegetable spray; form flattened biscuits around cups. Bake at 350 degrees for 14 minutes. Cool slightly and remove biscuit bowls from cups. Return to oven and bake 7 to 10 more minutes or until golden. Makes 8.

Anna McMaster
Portland, OR

Old-Fashioned Ham & Bean Soup

Start this soup a day ahead...it's just like Grandma used to make and well worth the wait!

16-oz. pkg. dried navy beans
2 meaty ham hocks or 1 meaty
    ham bone
1 c. cooked ham, chopped
½ to ¾ c. onion, quartered
    and sliced
3 stalks celery, chopped

½ c. carrot, peeled and grated
2 bay leaves
½ t. garlic powder
½ t. seasoned salt
¼ t. pepper
½ t. dried parsley
⅛ t. dried thyme

The night before, cover beans with water in a bowl and let stand overnight. The day before, cover ham hocks or ham bone with water in a large stockpot. Simmer over medium heat until tender. Remove ham hocks or bone from stockpot, reserving broth; slice off meat. Refrigerate reserved broth and meat overnight. The next day, drain beans and set aside. Discard fat from top of reserved broth; add beans, meat and remaining ingredients to broth. Bring to a boil. Reduce heat; simmer until beans are tender and soup is desired thickness, about one hour. Discard bay leaves. Serves 4 to 6.

Mary Beaney
Bourbonnais, IL

perfect pairings

Nothing goes better with hearty bean or pea soup than warm cornbread! If you like your cornbread crisp, prepare it in a vintage sectioned cast-iron skillet...each wedge of cornbread will bake up with its own golden crust.

Kielbasa & Veggie Soup

Perfect for lunch on a chilly day...pair this soup with warm, crusty bread.

2 T. butter
1-lb. pkg. Kielbasa, diced
1 onion, chopped
1 c. celery, peeled and chopped
5 c. water
2 c. carrots, sliced
4 to 5 c. beef broth
10¾-oz. can tomato soup
2 to 3 T. catsup
2 T. vinegar
1 bay leaf
½ t. dried thyme
1 T. salt
¾ t. pepper
2 c. potatoes, peeled and cubed

Heat butter in a Dutch oven over medium heat. Add Kielbasa, onion and celery; cook, stirring occasionally, until vegetables are tender. Add water and remaining ingredients except potatoes. Simmer, covered, over low heat one hour. Add potatoes and cook one more hour. Discard bay leaf. Serves 8 to 10.

Karen Puchnick
Butler, PA

This soup is a creation of mine after enjoying a Kielbasa soup at a local restaurant many moons ago.

Karen

put a lid on it

Keep a stockpot or slow-cooker lid where it belongs! Wrap a long, heavy-duty rubber band around a pot handle, twist it, and wrap over the lid and around the knob, then secure it to the handle on the other side.

Country Comfort
Chicken Soup

Country Comfort Chicken Soup

9 c. water
2 c. baby carrots, sliced
1 c. celery, chopped
2 T. garlic, minced
1½ t. seasoned salt
1 t. dried parsley
1 t. poultry seasoning

½ t. salt
¼ t. pepper
6 boneless, skinless chicken
    thighs
4 cubes chicken bouillon
5 c. fine egg noodles, uncooked

Place all ingredients except noodles in a large soup pot. Bring to a boil; cover, reduce heat and simmer until chicken and vegetables are tender, about one hour. Remove chicken from simmering broth; let chicken cool slightly. Stir noodles into broth; simmer, uncovered, until done, about 5 minutes. While noodles are cooking, dice chicken and return to soup. Serves 8.

South-of-the-Border Chicken Soup

Black beans and salsa add a Mexican flair to this filling soup that's a snap to make in the slow cooker.

2 to 3 boneless, skinless chicken
    breasts
15-oz. can black beans, drained
    and rinsed
15¼-oz. can corn, drained

24-oz. jar salsa
tortilla chips
Garnishes: sour cream, shredded
    Cheddar cheese

Layer chicken, beans, corn and salsa in a slow cooker. Cover and cook on low setting 6 to 8 hours or until chicken is done. Using 2 forks, shred chicken and return to slow cooker; ladle into bowls. Serve with chips and garnish with desired toppings. Serves 6 to 8.

Paula Lee
Lapel, IN

The ladies at church like this recipe because it's healthy and best of all...easy!

Paula

Slow-Cooker Taco Soup

Toss this soup in the slow cooker an hour before company arrives and use the extra time to make an appetizer or dessert!

1 lb. ground beef
1 onion, diced
1 clove garlic, minced
12-oz. bottle green taco sauce
4-oz. can green chiles, chopped
2 to 3 (15-oz.) cans black beans, drained and rinsed
15¼-oz. can corn, drained
15-oz. can tomato sauce
2 c. water
1¼-oz. pkg. taco seasoning mix
Garnishes: sour cream, shredded Cheddar cheese, corn chips

Brown beef, onion and garlic in a large skillet over medium heat; drain. In a slow cooker, combine beef mixture and remaining ingredients except garnishes. Cover and cook on high setting one hour. Serve with sour cream, shredded cheese and corn chips, if desired. Serves 8 to 10.

Susan Ahlstrand
Post Falls, ID

dress it up

Even garnishes can be dressed up. When you're sharing a pot of Slow-Cooker Taco Soup, line a new terra cotta pot with wax paper and shredded cheese, or add corn chips to a bandanna-lined sombrero...what fun!

Pastina Soup

This pasta-filled soup is best served with warm slices of Italian bread for dipping.

1 meaty beef shank bone
6 carrots, peeled and sliced
6 stalks celery, diced
2 onions, chopped
3 tomatoes, diced

salt and pepper to taste
16-oz. pkg. orzo pasta, uncooked
Garnish: grated Parmesan cheese

Cover beef shank bone with water in a Dutch oven; bring to a boil over medium heat. Add carrots, celery, onions, tomatoes, salt and pepper. Simmer over low heat 6 to 8 hours. Remove beef shank bone; cool and remove meat from bone. Add meat to soup; discard bone. In a separate pan, cook orzo 4 minutes; drain and add to soup. Simmer 5 more minutes. Sprinkle with Parmesan cheese, if desired. Serves 8.

Althea Paquette
South Attleboro, MA

This recipe is from my Italian grandmother. It's the easiest soup to make, and I think, the best!

Althea

trick-or-treat tradition

Start a delicious soup supper tradition on Halloween night. Soup stays simmering hot while you hand out treats, and it isn't too filling…everyone has more room to nibble on goodies!

Oven Beef Stew

This recipe is a lifesaver on busy days...just pop it in the oven and finish up your to-do list!

1½ lbs. stew beef, cubed
5 carrots, peeled and sliced
1 c. celery, chopped
2 onions, sliced
1 potato, peeled and chopped

2 (14.5-oz.) cans stewed
  tomatoes
½ c. soft bread crumbs
2 t. salt
3 T. instant tapioca, uncooked

Place beef, carrots, celery, onions and potato in a bowl. Combine remaining ingredients and add to beef mixture; blend well. Place in a greased 2½-quart Dutch oven. Cover and bake at 325 degrees for 4 hours. Serves 6.

Alice Monaghan
St. Joseph, MO

serving suggestion

When serving soups and stews, stack 2 or 3 cake stands, then fill each tier with a different type of roll for guests to try.

One-Pot Spicy Black Bean Chili

Serve this spicy dish with crunchy tortilla chips or a pan of warm cornbread.

1 onion, chopped
2 t. garlic, minced
2 t. olive oil
3 (16-oz.) cans black beans, drained and rinsed
16-oz. pkg. frozen corn
14½-oz. can tomatoes with chiles
2 c. water

1½ t. taco seasoning mix
7-oz. can chipotle chiles in adobo sauce
1 T. rice vinegar
¼ c. fresh cilantro, chopped
¼ c. sour cream
Optional: salsa, fresh cilantro sprigs

In a medium saucepan, sauté onion and garlic in oil over medium-high heat 5 to 7 minutes or until onion softens and begins to brown. Add beans, corn, tomatoes, water and taco seasoning mix. Bring to a boil; reduce heat to low and simmer 15 minutes, stirring occasionally. Combine chiles in sauce and vinegar in a blender; process until puréed. Stir chile mixture and cilantro into chili, adding more taco seasoning mix if a spicier chili is preferred; heat through. Divide among 4 soup bowls; top with dollops of sour cream. Garnish with salsa and a sprig of cilantro, if desired. Serves 4.

Lisanne Miller
Brandon, MS

Chili with Corn Dumplings

Dumplings created with cornmeal and fresh cilantro make this chili extra special and so satisfying.

4½ lbs. ground beef
2¼ c. chopped onion
3 (15-oz.) cans corn, undrained
   and divided
3 (14½-oz.) cans stewed
   tomatoes
3 (15-oz.) cans tomato sauce

1 T. hot pepper sauce
6 T. chili powder
1 T. garlic, minced
1⅓ c. biscuit baking mix
⅔ c. cornmeal
⅔ c. milk
3 T. fresh cilantro, chopped

Brown ground beef and onion in a Dutch oven over medium heat; drain. Set aside 1½ cups corn; stir remaining corn with liquid, tomatoes, sauces, chili powder and garlic into beef mixture. Bring to a boil. Reduce heat; cover and simmer 15 minutes. Combine baking mix and cornmeal in a medium bowl; stir in milk, cilantro and reserved corn just until moistened. Drop dough by rounded tablespoonfuls onto simmering chili. Cook over low heat, uncovered, 15 minutes. Cover and cook 15 to 18 more minutes or until dumplings are dry on top. Serves 10.

Tanya Graham
Lawrenceville, GA

Family Favorite Clam Chowder

Chase away those winter chills with this easy-to-make clam chowder.

3 to 4 c. potatoes, peeled
    and cubed
1 c. onion, diced
1 c. celery, diced
6½-oz. can minced clams,
    drained and juice reserved
8-oz. bottle clam juice

¾ c. butter
¾ c. all-purpose flour
1 qt. half-and-half
½ t. sugar
1½ t. salt
⅛ t. pepper

Place vegetables in a large saucepan; add reserved clam juice and bottled clam juice. Add just enough water to cover vegetables; bring to a boil over medium heat. Reduce heat; simmer, covered, until vegetables are tender, about 10 to 15 minutes. In a separate saucepan over medium heat, melt butter; whisk in flour and cook one minute. Add half-and-half, sugar, salt and pepper, whisking until smooth. Cook on low heat 3 to 4 minutes; stir into vegetable mixture. Heat through, 5 to 10 minutes. Serves 8.

Angie Whitmore
Farmington, UT

Crawfish-Corn Chowder

This tasty dish combines Louisiana crawfish with a hint of spice in a creamy chowder.

As displaced Cajuns from Lousiana now living in Texas, my family loves this chowder...it's a delicious reminder of home.

Becky

12-oz. pkg. bacon, crisply
    cooked, crumbled and
    drippings reserved
2 c. potatoes, peeled and diced
1 c. onion, diced
2 T. butter
2 pts. half-and-half

2 (16-oz.) cans creamed corn
1 T. Cajun seasoning
Optional: 1 t. hot pepper sauce
1 lb. frozen crawfish tails or
    uncooked medium shrimp,
    peeled and cleaned

Place ¼ cup reserved bacon drippings in a soup pot. Sauté potatoes and onion in drippings about 15 minutes or until golden. Stir in butter, half-and-half, corn, seasoning and hot pepper sauce, if desired. Add crumbled bacon to chowder. Cook over medium heat until potatoes are tender, about 20 to 30 minutes. Add crawfish or shrimp and simmer 15 to 20 more minutes; do not overcook shellfish. Serves 6 to 8.

Becky Garrett
Richardson, TX

Chicken Fajita Chowder
(pictured on page 315)

This quick & savory soup will be a new family favorite.

3 T. all-purpose flour
1-oz. pkg. fajita or taco
    seasoning mix, divided
4 boneless, skinless chicken
    breasts, cubed
3 T. oil
1 onion, chopped
1 t. minced garlic
15¼-oz. can sweet corn &
    diced peppers, drained
15-oz. can black beans,
    drained and rinsed

14½-oz. can Mexican-style
    stewed tomatoes
4-oz. can chopped green chiles
3 c. water
1 c. instant brown rice, uncooked
Optional: fresh cilantro to taste,
    chopped
10¾-oz. can nacho cheese soup
Garnishes: sour cream, shredded
    Cheddar cheese, chopped
    green onions, crushed
    tortilla chips

Combine flour and 2 tablespoons seasoning mix in a large plastic zipping bag; add chicken. Seal bag and shake to coat. Sauté chicken in oil in a large Dutch oven over high heat, stirring often, about 5 minutes or until golden. Reduce heat to medium-high. Add onion and garlic; sauté 5 minutes. Stir in remaining seasoning mix and all ingredients except soup and garnishes. Bring to a boil; reduce heat to medium-low, cover and simmer 5 minutes. Add soup; stir until heated through. Garnish as desired. Serves 8 to 10.

Kelly Jones
Tallahassee, FL

Red Barn Chowder

Enjoy the spicy taste of this delicious, hearty chowder filled with sausage and vegetables.

1 lb. ground hot Italian sausage, crumbled
1 onion, chopped
3 stalks celery, chopped
1 green pepper, chopped
1 red pepper, chopped
2 zucchini, quartered and sliced
3 to 4 cloves garlic, chopped
28-oz. can stewed tomatoes
10-oz. can tomatoes with chiles
6-oz. can tomato paste
1 c. water
2 t. dried basil
salt and pepper to taste
1 c. canned garbanzo beans, drained and rinsed

Combine sausage, onion, celery, peppers, zucchini and garlic in a large saucepan; sauté until sausage is browned and vegetables are tender. Stir in tomatoes, tomato paste, water, basil, salt and pepper; cook until heated through. Mix in garbanzo beans; heat through. Serves 8 to 10.

Suzanne Pottker
Elgin, IL

soup secret

Pre-warmed soup bowls are a thoughtful touch. Set oven-safe crocks on a baking sheet and tuck into a warm oven for a few minutes. Remove from oven and ladle in hot, hearty soup...mmm, pass the bread!

Easy as A, B, Seafood Bisque

Creamy seafood bisque is a cinch to make when you use prepared crab, lobster and shrimp.

6-oz. can crabmeat, drained
10-oz. pkg. imitation lobster, flaked
6-oz. can tiny shrimp, drained
½ c. plus 3 T. butter, divided
1 onion, chopped
1 carrot, peeled and chopped
1 stalk celery, chopped
14-oz. can chicken broth
Optional: ½ c. white wine
1 T. tomato paste
3 c. half-and-half
½ c. all-purpose flour
salt and pepper to taste
Garnish: fresh chives, chopped

Combine crabmeat, lobster and shrimp in a bowl; set aside. Melt 3 tablespoons butter in a large Dutch oven and sauté onion, carrot and celery about 3 minutes. Add chicken broth, seafood and wine, if desired. Bring to a boil; reduce heat and simmer. Stir in tomato paste and half-and-half. Melt remaining butter and blend with flour in a small bowl; stir into soup. Add salt and pepper. Simmer over low heat, stirring occasionally, 40 minutes. Garnish with chives, if desired. Serves 4 to 6.

Weda Mosellie
Phillipsburg, NJ

serving savvy

Add a bit of vintage charm to lunch…serve salads and soups in dainty teacups.

Curried Harvest Bisque

(pictured on page 166)

Top with ham for an elegant beginning to a holiday meal.

1 lb. butternut squash, peeled
    and cut into 1-inch cubes
5 c. chicken broth
¼ c. butter
¼ c. all-purpose flour
1 t. curry powder

¾ c. half-and-half
1 T. lime juice
½ t. salt
¼ t. white pepper
Garnish: diced ham

    Combine squash and broth in a heavy 4-quart stockpot. Cook over medium heat until squash is tender, about 15 minutes. Using a slotted spoon, transfer squash to a blender; purée until smooth. Stir broth back into puréed squash; set aside. Melt butter in stockpot; stir in flour and curry powder. Cook over medium heat, stirring, until smooth. Add squash mixture; increase heat to medium-high and stir until soup thickens slightly. Reduce heat to low; add remaining ingredients and heat through without boiling. Garnish, if desired. Serves 4.

Kathy Grashoff
Fort Wayne, IN

fall harvest

On warm fall days, set up tables and chairs outdoors for a soup supper. Decorate with plump pumpkins, bittersweet wreaths, straw bales and scarecrows. And before the sun sets, end the day with a hayride in the country.

Mom's Yummy Cornbread
Salad, page 224

scrumptious sides & salads

This selection of sides and salads makes rounding out your supper or putting together a yummy one-dish meal a snap. Try Green Bean Bundles (page 199) for an elegant side dish when you have company coming to supper. Classic Baked Macaroni & Cheese (page 216) is a comfort food favorite that your whole family will love. And Spinach Salad & Hot Bacon Dressing (page 227) pairs well with just about any entrée. With so many delicious recipes to choose from, there's something here for everyone!

Sesame Asparagus

For best results, use an iron skillet. Serve chilled with a dash of fresh lemon juice.

2 T. peanut oil
1 lb. asparagus, trimmed
2 T. shallots, minced
1 T. sesame seed

2 t. soy sauce
¼ t. pepper
⅛ t. lemon juice

Heat oil in a skillet over medium-high heat; add asparagus in a single layer. Cook asparagus about 4 minutes; turn and cook 3 more minutes. Asparagus will be slightly browned. Add shallots and sesame seed; cook, tossing the asparagus in the mixture, until shallots are transparent. Add soy sauce and pepper. Transfer to a serving dish and sprinkle with lemon juice. Serves 4.

keep it fresh

Asparagus is best when eaten freshly picked. You can store it for a few days in the refrigerator wrapped in a plastic bag. Don't clean until ready to cook.

Garden-Fresh Green Beans

This recipe is such a treat made with the first green beans, peppers and tomatoes of the season.

4 to 6 slices smoked bacon,
    diced
2 lbs. green beans, trimmed
1 onion, diced

1 green bell pepper, diced
1 tomato, diced
salt and pepper to taste

In a large heavy skillet over medium heat, cook bacon until crisp. Remove bacon, reserving drippings in skillet. Add remaining ingredients to skillet. Cover tightly and reduce heat to low; cook 10 minutes. Add just enough water to cover bottom of skillet; increase heat to medium and cook until beans are tender. Stir in cooked bacon. Serves 8.

Vickie Fallis
Osgood, IN

This recipe came from a cookbook from the 1940s.

Vickie

Green Bean Bundles

Easy and delicious! The most obvious timesaver in this recipe is to not make the bundles, but it is definitely worth the effort.

3 (14½-oz.) cans whole green
    beans, drained
8 slices bacon, cut in half
    crosswise

6 T. butter, melted
½ c. brown sugar, packed
2 to 3 cloves garlic, minced

Gather beans in bundles of 10; wrap each bundle with a half-slice of bacon. Arrange bundles in a lightly greased 13"x 9" baking pan. Mix melted butter, sugar and garlic in a small bowl; spoon over bundles. Cover and bake at 375 degrees for 30 minutes. Uncover and bake 15 more minutes. Serves 8.

Wendy Sensing
Brentwood, TN

This is one of our favorite side dishes to bring to church get-togethers. The pan always comes home empty and someone always wants the recipe, especially the garlic lovers.

Wendy

perfect potatoes

Turn leftover mashed potatoes into twice-baked potatoes. Stir in minced onion, crumbled bacon and shredded cheese to taste; pat into individual ramekins. Bake at 350 degrees until hot and golden…delicious!

Ham & Lima Bean Pot

This dish is unbelievably good…an absolute must for warming up on a brisk day. So nice to tote to a church supper, too.

1½ c. dried lima beans
6 c. water
1 c. cooked ham, diced
1 onion, chopped
⅓ c. molasses

⅓ c. chili sauce
1 T. vinegar
1 t. dry mustard
⅛ t. cayenne pepper

Combine beans and water in a stockpot; let stand overnight. Drain beans; add 6 cups fresh water. Simmer over low heat 1½ hours. Drain again, reserving one cup liquid. Combine cooked beans, reserved liquid and remaining ingredients. Mix well and spread in a lightly greased 2-quart casserole dish. Bake, uncovered, at 350 degrees for 30 minutes or until golden. Serves 4 to 6.

LaVerne Fang
Joliet, IL

Broccoli with Orange Sauce

Good ol' broccoli...all dressed up for the holidays or any day!

1 lb. broccoli, cut into spears
1 T. cornstarch
1 c. orange juice, divided
2 T. butter
1 T. fresh parsley, minced
1 T. lemon juice
1 T. orange zest
½ t. dried thyme
½ t. dry mustard
¼ t. pepper
Garnish: orange slices or
orange zest

Place broccoli in a large saucepan with about one inch of water. Bring to a boil over medium heat; cook 7 minutes or just until tender. In a bowl, combine cornstarch and ½ cup orange juice, stirring until blended. In a separate saucepan, melt butter; add cornstarch mixture, remaining orange juice and remaining ingredients except garnish. Cook over medium heat until mixture thickens. Pour over broccoli. Garnish as desired. Serves 4.

Glazed Carrots

(pictured on page 308)

Carrots add a cheerful, bright splash of color and flavor to any meal.

2 T. onion, chopped
2 T. fresh parsley, chopped
2 T. butter
8 carrots, peeled and quartered
10½-oz. can beef broth
¼ t. sugar
Optional: nutmeg

In a skillet over medium heat, sauté onion and parsley in butter until onion is tender. Add carrots, broth and sugar. Cover and cook 5 minutes. Uncover and cook 10 more minutes or until carrots are crisp-tender. Sprinkle with a little nutmeg, if desired. Serves 8.

Kickin' Chili Fries

Hearty chili and melted cheese over French fries...yum!

32-oz. pkg. frozen French fries
15-oz. can chili without beans

8-oz. jar pasteurized process
  cheese sauce

Fry or bake French fries according to package directions; place on a serving platter and keep warm. Heat chili and cheese sauce separately, according to package directions. Spoon hot chili over fries; top with hot cheese sauce and serve immediately. Serves 8.

Colleen Lambert
Casco, WI

terra cotta trick

New, unused terra cotta pots make super summer serving dishes. Line a pot with a tea towel, napkin or bandanna and fill it with fresh veggies, rolls, bread sticks, straws or silverware.

Buffalo Potato Wedges

These potatoes are irresistible as either a side dish or an appetizer.

6 to 8 potatoes, sliced into
   wedges
1 to 2 T. olive oil
salt, pepper and garlic
   powder to taste

¼ c. butter
½ c. hot pepper sauce
Optional: blue cheese
   salad dressing

Arrange potato wedges on a baking sheet sprayed with non-stick vegetable spray. Drizzle with oil; sprinkle with salt, pepper and garlic powder. Bake at 375 degrees for about 30 minutes or until tender, tossing occasionally. Remove pan from oven. Combine butter and hot sauce in a microwave-safe bowl. Microwave on high until butter is melted, about one minute; mix well. Drizzle butter mixture over potato wedges; bake 15 more minutes. If desired, serve with salad dressing for dipping. Serves 8 to 10.

Victoria Francis
McHenry, IL

easy buffet

Serve up a festive sandwich buffet for an oh-so-easy gathering. Set out a savory selection of deli meats, cheeses, breads and other fixin's for make-your-own-sandwiches...even gourmet mustards. Add a tabletop grill for making hot sandwiches, then just relax and enjoy your guests.

Auntie Ruth's Potatoes

To keep this dish warm, place it in a 200-degree oven until ready to serve.

2 T. butter
2 slices bacon, crisply cooked,
    crumbled and drippings
    reserved
4 potatoes, peeled and
    thinly sliced

1 T. onion, diced
2 eggs
salt and pepper to taste
½ c. shredded Cheddar cheese

Always a breakfast "must-have" when family visits for the holidays.

Dana

Melt butter with reserved bacon drippings in skillet. Add potatoes and onion; cover and cook over medium heat, stirring occasionally, until potatoes are golden and tender. Reduce heat; crack eggs over potatoes and stir gently. Sprinkle with salt, pepper, cheese and crumbled bacon. Cook over low heat until eggs are firm and cheese melts. Serves 4.

Dana Cunningham
Lafayette, LA

Creamy Potatoes Au Gratin

Warm & cheesy…these potatoes are always everyone's favorite.

4 russet potatoes, peeled,
    sliced ¼-inch thick
    and divided
1 onion, thinly sliced
salt and pepper to taste
3 T. butter

3 T. all-purpose flour
½ t. salt
2 c. milk
2 c. shredded Cheddar cheese,
    divided

Arrange half the potato slices in a greased 1½-quart casserole dish. Top with onion and remaining potatoes; add salt and pepper to taste. In a medium saucepan, melt butter over medium heat. Add flour and salt; stir constantly with a whisk one minute. Stir in milk; cook until thickened. Stir in 1½ cups cheese; continue to stir until melted. Pour over potatoes; cover with aluminum foil. Bake at 400 degrees for one hour. Uncover; sprinkle with remaining cheese. Bake 10 to 15 more minutes or until lightly browned. Serves 4.

Tami Bowman
Marysville, OH

Sour Cream Mashed Potatoes

Fluffy mashed potatoes are topped with sour cream and bacon and baked golden brown…irresistible!

5 lbs. russet or Yukon Gold
   potatoes, peeled and cubed
2 T. butter
1 c. sour cream

salt and pepper to taste
4 slices bacon, crisply cooked
   and crumbled

Cover potatoes with cold salted water in a large saucepan. Bring to a boil; simmer 20 minutes or until tender. Drain and mash with a potato masher or ricer. Whisk in butter and sour cream; add salt and pepper. Sprinkle with crumbled bacon; transfer to a greased 13"x9" baking pan. Bake, uncovered, at 350 degrees for 10 to 15 minutes. Serves 10.

charming centerpiece

A rustic metal watering can makes a charming centerpiece filled with stems of cutting-garden favorites like silver dollar plant, Chinese lanterns and bells of Ireland.

Fruity Roasted Sweet Potatoes

With the addition of apples and cranberries, these sweet potatoes define comfort food.

3 sweet potatoes, peeled and
    cubed
2 Granny Smith apples, cored,
    peeled and cubed
2 T. olive oil
1 c. fresh cranberries
1 T. honey

1½ T. brown sugar, packed
1½ T. chopped walnuts
¼ c. sweetened flaked coconut
1 t. ground ginger
1 t. cinnamon
¼ t. salt

Combine potatoes, apples and oil in a lightly greased 13"x9" baking pan. Mix well. Sprinkle cranberries on top of potato mixture and drizzle with honey. Bake, uncovered, at 450 degrees for 10 minutes. Reduce heat to 350 degrees and bake 45 to 50 more minutes, or until potatoes are tender. Mix together brown sugar and remaining ingredients. Remove casserole from oven and sprinkle brown sugar mixture over top. Bake 5 more minutes. Serves 4 to 6.

Becca Brasfield
Burns, TN

Stuffed Pepper Wedges

These peppers are also an impressive, easy-to-prepare appetizer...and a real crowd pleaser.

In summer, I make these quite often using red, yellow and green peppers fresh from my garden.

Kathleen

½ c. chive & onion cream
    cheese spread
1 T. black olives, chopped

2 green, red or yellow peppers,
    sliced into 8 wedges each
¼ c. shredded Cheddar cheese

Mix cream cheese and olives together in a small bowl. Spread about 2 teaspoons of mixture onto each pepper wedge; sprinkle with cheese. Arrange peppers on an aluminum foil-lined baking sheet. Broil in oven 6 to 8 minutes or until cheese is melted and peppers begin to char slightly. Serve warm or cold. Makes 16.

Kathleen Felton
Fairfax, IA

Creamy Butternut Squash

Carrots and onion add extra flavor to this classic fall side dish.

2 lbs. butternut squash, peeled
    and cubed
10¾-oz. can cream of
    chicken soup
8-oz. container sour cream

⅓ c. butter, melted
2 carrots, peeled and shredded
½ c. onion, chopped
2¼ c. herb-flavored stuffing
    mix, divided

Place squash and a small amount of water in a saucepan. Simmer over medium heat 3 minutes; drain well and set aside. Combine soup, sour cream, butter, carrots and onion in a large bowl; stir in 2 cups stuffing mix. Fold in squash; transfer to a greased 11"x7" baking pan. Sprinkle with remaining stuffing mix. Bake, uncovered, at 350 degrees for 45 minutes. Serves 4 to 6.

Rebecca Cook
San Antonio, TX

squash carving

When it comes to preparing squash, try using the knife that comes in a pumpkin-carving kit...its small size is just right for slicing squash!

Country-Fried Green Tomatoes

Country-Fried Green Tomatoes

These are a must-have side dish in the summer when green tomatoes are plentiful in the garden.

1 c. buttermilk
1 egg, beaten
1 c. cornmeal
½ c. all-purpose flour
2 T. sugar

⅛ t. salt
¼ t. pepper
2 to 3 green tomatoes,
    sliced ½-inch thick
vegetable oil for frying

Whisk together buttermilk and egg in a shallow bowl. Combine cornmeal, flour, sugar, salt and pepper in another shallow bowl. Dip tomato slices into buttermilk mixture; coat in cornmeal mixture. Heat oil, about one-inch deep, in a large skillet over medium-high heat. Cook tomatoes 4 minutes on each side or until golden. Serves 4.

Angie Stone
Argillite, KY

Tangy Tomato Slices

Few things are more scrumptious than a ripe fresh tomato.

6 tomatoes, thinly sliced
1 onion, thinly sliced
1 c. olive oil
⅓ c. vinegar
¼ c. fresh parsley, chopped
3 T. fresh basil, chopped

1 T. sugar
1 t. salt
½ t. pepper
½ t. dry mustard
½ t. garlic powder

Layer tomato and onion slices in a greased 13"x9" baking pan; set aside. Combine oil, vinegar and remaining ingredients in a small bowl; mix well and pour over tomatoes and onions. Cover and chill 4 to 5 hours. Serves 6 to 8.

Jennifer Eveland-Kupp
Blandon, PA

Golden Zucchini Patties

Not the "usual" zucchini patties, these have an amazing flavor and bake up golden and delicious.

3½ c. zucchini, grated
3 T. onion, grated
2 T. fresh parsley, minced
⅓ c. grated Parmesan cheese
1 c. soft bread crumbs

1 t. salt
½ t. pepper
2 eggs, beaten
¾ c. dry bread crumbs
½ c. butter, melted

Wrap zucchini in paper towels; press out as much liquid as possible. Combine zucchini, onion, parsley, cheese, soft bread crumbs, salt, pepper and eggs. Shape zucchini mixture into patties; dip each patty into dry bread crumbs. Place on greased baking sheets; drizzle each patty with butter. Bake at 350 degrees for 30 to 40 minutes or until golden. Serves 6 to 8.

Edie DeSpain
Logan, UT

Spanish Rice

Pair this hearty side dish with chicken, steak or Mexican favorites like tacos and enchiladas.

1½ lbs. ground beef
2 (10¾-oz.) cans tomato soup
¼ c. green pepper, chopped

Optional: ¼ c. onion, chopped
1½ c. instant rice, cooked

Brown ground beef in a large skillet over medium heat; drain. Add tomato soup, green pepper and onion, if desired; mix well. Add rice, stirring gently. Simmer 15 minutes. Serves 8 to 10.

Bobbi Crosson
Toledo, OH

get the dish

When deciding on a dish to share, keep in mind the recipes that are made just for simmering all day in a slow cooker, or ones that are a snap to reheat in the oven or microwave.

When my three sons were little, they asked me to make this for our church potlucks...that way they knew there would be something there that they liked. My youngest son, now thirty-five, called me for this recipe a couple of weeks ago.

Bobbi

Classic Baked Macaroni & Cheese

(pictured on cover)

It's worth shredding the cheese yourself for this classic dish. A sprinkle of pepper adds a surprise kick. For one-pot macaroni and cheese, prepare recipe as directed, stirring all shredded cheese into thickened milk mixture until melted. Stir in cooked pasta, salt and peppers, and serve immediately.

8-oz. pkg. elbow macaroni
2 T. butter
2 T. all-purpose flour
2 c. milk
8-oz. block sharp Cheddar
 cheese, shredded and
 divided

1 t. salt
½ t. freshly ground black pepper
¼ t. cayenne pepper

Prepare macaroni according to package directions. Keep warm. Melt butter in a large saucepan or Dutch oven over medium-low heat; whisk in flour until smooth. Cook, whisking constantly, 2 minutes. Gradually whisk in milk and cook, whisking constantly, 5 minutes or until thickened. Remove from heat. Stir in one cup shredded cheese, salt, peppers and cooked macaroni. Spoon into 4 lightly greased 8-ounce oven-proof ramekins; top with remaining one cup cheese. Bake at 400 degrees for 15 minutes or until bubbly. Let stand 10 minutes before serving. Serves 4.

Mac & Cheese Nuggets

Little kids really go for these cheesy morsels...big kids do, too!

¼ c. grated Parmesan cheese,
    divided
1½ T. butter
2 T. all-purpose flour
¾ c. milk
1¼ c. shredded Cheddar cheese

¼ lb. American cheese slices,
    chopped
1 egg yolk, beaten
¼ t. paprika
8-oz. pkg. elbow macaroni,
    cooked

Lightly grease mini muffin cups. Sprinkle with 2 tablespoons Parmesan cheese, tapping out excess. Melt butter in a large saucepan over medium heat. Stir in flour; cook 2 minutes. Whisk in milk and stir until boiling, about 5 minutes. Add Cheddar and American cheeses; remove from heat and stir until smooth. Whisk in egg yolk and paprika; fold in macaroni until well coated. Spoon rounded tablespoons of macaroni mixture into prepared cups; sprinkle with remaining Parmesan cheese. Bake at 425 degrees for about 10 minutes or until hot and golden. Cool 5 minutes; carefully transfer to a serving plate. Makes 4 dozen.

Vickie
Gooseberry Patch

Picnic Salad Skewers

What a fun way to pack a salad! For a meal-in-one version, slide on some cubes of Cheddar cheese and cold cuts, too.

8 redskin potatoes
8 pearl onions, peeled
1 green pepper, cut into
    1-inch squares
1 red or yellow bell pepper,
    cut into 1-inch squares

16 cherry tomatoes
1 zucchini, sliced ¼-inch thick
8 wooden skewers
Vinaigrette
Optional: 4-oz. container
    crumbled feta cheese

Cover potatoes with water in a saucepan; bring to a boil over medium heat. Cook 10 to 13 minutes, adding onions after 5 minutes; drain and cool. Thread all vegetables alternately onto skewers. Arrange skewers in a large shallow plastic container. Drizzle with Vinaigrette. Cover and refrigerate at least one hour, turning frequently. Sprinkle with cheese before serving, if desired. Serves 8.

Vinaigrette:

⅔ c. olive oil
⅓ c. red wine vinegar
2 cloves garlic, minced

1 T. dried oregano
1 t. salt
¼ t. pepper

Whisk together all ingredients. Makes about one cup.

Pam James
Gooseberry Patch

Rice Pilaf with Carrots

You'll find this rice dish to be delicious, easy and perfect with chicken dishes!

1 T. vegetable oil
2 c. basmati rice, uncooked
¼ c. onion, chopped
2 cloves garlic, minced
4 c. chicken broth

½ t. salt
1 c. carrots, finely chopped
½ c. green onions, chopped
3 T. pine nuts, toasted

Heat oil in a medium saucepan over medium-high heat. Add rice and onion; sauté 2 minutes. Add garlic; sauté one minute. Add broth and salt; bring to a boil. Cover, reduce heat and simmer 7 minutes. Stir in carrots; cover and cook 7 more minutes or until liquid is absorbed. Remove from heat; stir in remaining ingredients. Let stand, covered, 5 minutes, then fluff with a fork. Serves 6 to 8.

Minted Pea Salad

Prepare this dish to serve immediately, or refrigerate and serve later... very versatile!

4 c. fresh peas, blanched, or
    16-oz. pkg. frozen peas,
    thawed
¼ lb. sliced smoked deli ham,
    chopped

½ c. fresh mint, chopped
½ c. mayonnaise
¼ c. rice wine vinegar
1 t. fresh dill, chopped

Combine peas, ham and mint in a mixing bowl. In another bowl, combine mayonnaise, vinegar and dill. Add dressing to pea mixture and toss together. Serves 4 to 6.

Summer Tortellini Salad

(pictured on page 312)

Include any of your favorite veggies...a garnish of tomato wedges and basil leaves makes a nice presentation.

8-oz. pkg. cheese tortellini, cooked and cooled
1 tomato, chopped
3 to 4 slices hard salami, thinly sliced lengthwise
3 to 4 mushrooms, sliced
4 to 5 Kalamata olives, pitted and chopped
½ c. mild Cheddar cheese, cubed
½ c. mozzarella cheese, cubed
½ c. provolone cheese, cubed
¼ c. olive oil
1 clove garlic, finely minced
¼ t. garlic salt
⅛ t. pepper
2 to 3 T. cider vinegar
Optional: 1 t. red pepper flakes

In a large bowl, combine tortellini, tomato, salami, mushrooms, olives and cheeses; set aside. Whisk together oil, garlic, garlic salt, pepper, vinegar and red pepper flakes, if desired, until thoroughly mixed. Pour dressing over salad; mix well. Refrigerate for a few hours to blend flavors. Mix well again before serving. Serves 4 to 6.

Jen Eveland-Kupp
Blandon, PA

Fried Okra Salad

The okra soaks up all the yummy sweet vinaigrette in this salad...a nice contrast to the crunchy bacon.

2-lb. pkg. frozen breaded
   okra
10 slices bacon, crisply cooked
   and crumbled
6 roma tomatoes, chopped

1 bunch green onions,
   chopped
½ c. olive oil
¼ c. sugar
2 T. vinegar

Fry okra according to package directions; drain. Combine okra, bacon, tomatoes and green onions; set aside. Mix together remaining ingredients; pour dressing over okra mixture. Best served at room temperature. Serve immediately. Serves 8.

Lisa Martin
Tulsa, OK

I took this dish to a ladies' function at my church and by the time it was over, everyone had copied the recipe!

Lisa

get ready, get set

Instead of setting up one or two long dining tables, scatter several smaller ones around the room so friends can chat easily.

Mom's Yummy Cornbread Salad

(pictured on page 194)

This salad disappears from the table so quickly…you might want to double the recipe!

Mom was a great cook, and it makes me feel close to her when I prepare her recipes. When I compiled a family cookbook recently, this recipe was a must-have.

Denise

1 to 2 c. cornbread, cubed
8¾-oz. can corn, drained
½ c. green onions, chopped
½ c. cucumber, chopped
½ c. broccoli, chopped
½ c. red pepper, chopped
½ c. tomato, chopped

½ c. canned pinto or garbanzo
  beans, drained and rinsed
½ c. shredded Cheddar cheese
½ c. buttermilk ranch salad
  dressing
½ t. salt
½ t. pepper

Combine all ingredients in a large bowl. Gently mix and cover. Best when refrigerated at least 4 hours before serving. Serves 6.

Denise Neal
Castle Rock, CO

Mother's Cucumber Salad

Cool, crisp, not to mention delicious, this salad tastes even better the longer it marinates in the refrigerator.

3 to 4 cucumbers, peeled
    and thinly sliced
3 T. salt
2 t. sugar
½ t. onion powder

¼ t. celery seed
¼ t. pepper
¼ c. cider vinegar
Optional: ½ c. sliced red
    onion

This is my mother's recipe...it always reminds me of summer and picnics.

Amy

    Place cucumbers in a large bowl; add salt and enough water to cover. Cover and gently shake to mix. Refrigerate several hours to overnight. Drain cucumbers but do not rinse; return to bowl. Combine sugar, onion powder, celery seed, pepper and vinegar in a small bowl; mix well. Pour vinegar mixture over cucumbers. Add onion, if desired. Cover and shake gently to mix. Serves 6.

Amy Gerhart
Farmington, MI

picnic perfect

Tote a picnic lunch in style…in a one-of-a-kind bicycle basket! It's easy to make using a lidded container or a paper maché box from a craft store. Simply attach stickers, glue on ribbons or decorate the container with acrylic paints. When the "basket" is done, punch holes in the back, thread lengths of ribbon through the holes and tie onto the handlebars with bows.

Spinach Salad & Hot Bacon Dressing

The hot & savory dressing is the key ingredient to this salad's fantastic taste.

10-oz. bag spinach, torn into
    bite-size pieces
4 eggs, hard-boiled, peeled
    and sliced
1 tomato, chopped
1 red onion, sliced
8 to 10 large mushrooms,
    sliced
Hot Bacon Dressing

Toss all ingredients together; serve with Hot Bacon Dressing. Serves 4.

Hot Bacon Dressing:

1 lb. bacon, cut into
    1-inch pieces
1 onion, chopped
1 clove garlic, minced
½ c. brown sugar, packed
½ c. red wine vinegar
2 c. water, divided
¼ t. salt
½ t. pepper
1 T. cornstarch

In a large skillet, sauté bacon, onion and garlic until bacon is crisp. Add brown sugar, vinegar, 1½ cups water, salt and pepper; simmer until mixture cooks down by half. In a bowl, mix together cornstarch and remaining water; add to pan and simmer until thick and bubbly. Makes 2 cups.

Kristie Rigo
Friedens, PA

Skillet-Toasted Corn Salad

The corn for this salad is cooked until toasty brown and tossed with peppers and Parmesan cheese...yummy!

⅓ c. plus 1 T. olive oil, divided
⅓ c. lemon juice
1 T. Worcestershire sauce
3 cloves garlic, minced
3 to 4 dashes hot pepper sauce
¼ t. salt
½ t. pepper

6 ears sweet corn, husks and kernels removed
4 red, yellow and green peppers, coarsely chopped
½ c. grated Parmesan cheese
1 head romaine lettuce, cut crosswise into 1-inch pieces

In a jar with a tight-fitting lid, combine ⅓ cup oil, lemon juice, Worcestershire sauce, garlic, hot pepper sauce, salt and pepper. Cover and shake well; set aside. Heat remaining oil in a large skillet over medium-high heat. Add corn kernels; sauté 5 minutes or until corn is tender and golden, stirring often. Remove from heat; keep warm. Combine corn, peppers and cheese in a large bowl. Pour dressing over corn mixture; toss lightly to coat. Serve over lettuce. Serves 6 to 8.

Sherri Cooper
Armada, MI

Whenever my father comes to visit, this salad is one that he requests. He usually stops by the local farmers' vegetable stand on his way to our house and picks up fresh ears of corn... just for this salad!

Sherri

Waldorf Slaw

Everyone will love this tangy salad that's easily made ahead.

16-oz. pkg. coleslaw mix
2 c. Braeburn apples, cored,
    peeled and chopped
1 c. Bartlett pears, cored,
    peeled and chopped
½ c. raisins
3 T. chopped walnuts

½ c. mayonnaise
½ c. buttermilk
1 t. lemon zest
2 T. lemon juice
¼ t. salt
⅛ t. pepper

Combine coleslaw, apples, pears, raisins and walnuts in a large bowl; set aside. Combine remaining ingredients, stirring well with a whisk. Drizzle mayonnaise mixture over coleslaw mixture and toss to coat. Cover and refrigerate 30 minutes. Serves 10.

Lori Rosenberg
University Heights, OH

No-Knead Oatmeal Bread,
page 238

best-loved breads

Use this collection of recipes to fill your home with the aroma of freshly baked bread. Discover the pleasure of waking up to a delicious batch of Cheese Danish Rolls (page 241). Or bake a loaf of Perfect Lemon Bread (page 245) to welcome a new neighbor or as a treat for a dear friend. When dinnertime rolls around, share your bounty with Kit's Herbed Bread (page 251) or Melt-In-Your-Mouth Biscuits (page 253). Find yeast breads and quick breads that are so yummy you'll want to start baking now!

Holiday Cloverleaf Rolls

You can double this recipe and freeze any extra rolls. These are great for breakfast, warmed in the microwave and topped with homemade jam.

4 to 5 c. all-purpose flour,
    divided
⅓ c. sugar
1 t. salt
2 pkgs. instant dry yeast

½ c. water
½ c. milk
½ c. butter, melted and
    divided
2 eggs

In a large mixing bowl, combine one cup flour, sugar, salt and yeast. In a medium saucepan over low heat, heat water, milk and ¼ cup butter until warm (110 to 115 degrees). Gradually pour liquid into dry ingredients, beating at low speed with an electric mixer. Increase speed to medium; beat 2 minutes, occasionally scraping bowl with rubber spatula. Add eggs and enough flour to make a thick batter. Continue beating 2 minutes, occasionally scraping bowl. With a spoon, stir in enough additional flour to make a soft dough. Turn dough onto a floured surface and knead 10 minutes or until dough is smooth and elastic. Shape dough into a ball and place in a large greased bowl, turning to coat. Cover with a towel; let rise in a warm place (85 degrees), away from drafts, one hour or until doubled in bulk. Punch down dough in the center, then push edges of dough into center. Turn dough onto a floured surface; cut in half. Cover with a towel 15 minutes. Grease 24 (2- to 3-inch) muffin cups. With a sharp knife or kitchen shears, cut half of dough into 36 equal pieces. Shape each piece into a smooth ball. Place 3 balls into each muffin cup. Brush tops with remaining melted butter. Cover with a towel; let rise in a warm place 45 minutes or until doubled in bulk. Repeat with second half of dough. Remove towel from rolls and bake at 400 degrees for 10 to 15 minutes or until golden. Makes 2 dozen.

Kathy Schroeder
Riverside, CA

Butterhorn Rolls

Start making these delicious buttery treats the night before and roll them out a few hours before serving...they will melt in your mouth!

1 pkg. active dry yeast
½ c. plus 1 T. sugar, divided
1 c. plus ¼ c. warm water,
    divided

¾ c. butter, melted and divided
1 t. salt
3 eggs, lightly beaten
5 c. all-purpose flour

In a large bowl, dissolve yeast and one tablespoon sugar in ¼ cup warm water (110 to 115 degrees). Add one cup warm water and ½ cup butter to yeast mixture. Combine yeast mixture, ½ cup sugar, salt and eggs. Add flour, one cup at a time, mixing well. Cover and refrigerate overnight. Remove dough from refrigerator 3 hours before serving. Roll out into a ⅛-inch-thick circle on a heavily floured surface and spread top of dough with remaining ¼ cup melted butter. Cut into wedges like a pie. Roll up each wedge, starting at larger end. Place on a greased baking sheet, cover with a cloth and let rise in a warm place (85 degrees), away from drafts, until doubled in bulk (about 20 minutes). Remove cloth; brush with remaining melted butter. Bake at 375 degrees for 12 to 15 minutes. Makes 16 rolls.

Francie Stutzman
Dayton, OH

dough know-how

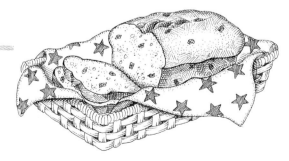

To know when rising dough has doubled in size, press two fingertips into the dough, about ½-inch deep, and then release. If the dent remains, the dough has doubled.

That Yummy Bread

Homemade bread with a savory herb filling...unforgettable!

1 c. milk	2 pkgs. active dry yeast
2 T. sugar	7 c. all-purpose flour, divided
¼ c. shortening	2 eggs, beaten and divided
2½ t. salt	Herb Filling
1 c. water	1 to 2 T. butter, melted

In a medium saucepan, heat milk just to boiling; stir in sugar, shortening and salt. Cool to lukewarm and set aside. Heat water until warm (110 to 115 degrees); add yeast, stir to dissolve and add to milk mixture. Pour into a large bowl and add 4 cups flour; stir and beat. Gradually add remaining flour; stir. Let dough rest 10 minutes; turn dough out onto a floured surface and knead until smooth. Place dough in a greased bowl, turning to coat. Cover and let rise in a warm place (85 degrees), away from drafts, until doubled in bulk. Punch down dough; shape into 2 balls. Roll out each ball into a ¼-inch-thick 15"x9" rectangle. Brush with 2 tablespoons egg, reserving remainder for filling. Spread Herb Filling to one inch from edges of dough; roll up jelly-roll style, starting at short edge. Pinch edges to seal; place in 2 greased 9"x5" loaf pans, seam-side down. Brush with butter; cover and let rise in a warm place 55 minutes. Slash tops of loaves with a knife; bake at 375 degrees for one hour. Let cool before slicing. Makes 2 loaves.

Herb Filling:

2 c. fresh parsley, chopped	¾ t. salt
2 c. green onions, chopped	pepper and hot pepper
1 clove garlic, minced	sauce to taste
2 T. butter	

Sauté parsley, onions and garlic in butter; cool slightly and add reserved egg from main recipe. Add salt, pepper and hot pepper sauce.

Francie Stutzman
Dayton, OH

No-Knead Oatmeal Bread

(pictured on page 232)

Spread peanut butter or softened butter on this slightly sweet and so-yummy favorite.

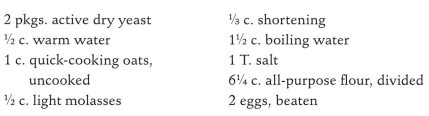

I've been making this bread since I was a little girl.

Hattie

2 pkgs. active dry yeast
½ c. warm water
1 c. quick-cooking oats, uncooked
½ c. light molasses
⅓ c. shortening
1½ c. boiling water
1 T. salt
6¼ c. all-purpose flour, divided
2 eggs, beaten

In a small bowl, dissolve yeast in warm water (110 to 115 degrees); let stand about 5 minutes. In a large bowl, combine oats, molasses, shortening, boiling water and salt; stir until shortening is melted. Cool until lukewarm. Stir in 2 cups flour; add eggs and beat well. Stir in yeast mixture. Add remaining flour, 2 cups at a time, mixing well after each addition to make a rather stiff dough. Beat vigorously until smooth, about 10 minutes. Grease top of dough lightly. Cover tightly; place in refrigerator at least 2 hours to overnight. Turn dough out onto a floured surface. Form into 2 loaves; place seam-side down in greased 8"x4" loaf pans. Cover; let rise in a warm place (85 degrees), away from drafts, 2 hours or until doubled in bulk. Bake at 375 degrees for about 40 minutes. If top begins to brown too fast, cover with aluminum foil for last half of baking time. Makes 2 loaves.

Hattie Douthit
Crawford, NE

Orange-Cinnamon Swirl Bread

A slice of this sweet & spicy bread is a perfect pick-me-up on those cold and dreary days!

5½ c. all-purpose flour, divided
2 pkgs. active dry yeast
⅓ c. dry powdered milk
1 c. sugar, divided
1½ t. salt
1¼ c. warm water
¼ c. butter, softened

1 T. plus 1 t. orange zest, divided
¾ c. plus 4 t. orange juice, divided
1 egg, beaten
1 T. cinnamon
1 c. powdered sugar

In a large mixing bowl, combine 2 cups flour, yeast, dry milk, ½ cup sugar and salt. Pour in warm water (110 to 115 degrees) and blend into a thin batter. Add butter, one tablespoon orange zest, ¾ cup orange juice and egg. Add remaining flour, ¼ cup at a time, until dough forms a ball that comes away from the sides of the bowl. Knead 8 minutes. Place dough in a greased bowl and cover tightly with plastic wrap. Let rise in a warm place (85 degrees), away from drafts, 45 minutes. Remove plastic wrap and punch dough down. Turn onto a floured surface and divide into 2 pieces. Roll each piece into a 15"x7" rectangle. In a small bowl, combine remaining ½ cup sugar and cinnamon; spread each dough rectangle with cinnamon mixture. Roll up dough jelly-roll style, starting at short side, and pinch seams together. Place in 2 greased 9"x5" loaf pans, cover with wax paper and let rise in a warm place 45 minutes. Bake at 375 degrees for 10 minutes; reduce heat to 325 degrees and bake 30 more minutes. In a large bowl, blend together powdered sugar, remaining orange zest and orange juice; set aside. Remove bread from oven, turn onto a wire rack and let cool. Spread frosting evenly over the top of each loaf. Makes 2 loaves.

Patty Rogers
Chicago, IL

Dakota Bread

This hearty bread is named for all the good grains in it, which are grown in the Dakotas.

1 pkg. active dry yeast
½ c. warm water
½ c. cottage cheese
¼ c. honey
1 egg
2 T. oil
1 t. salt
2¼ c. bread flour, divided

½ c. whole-wheat flour
¼ c. wheat germ, toasted
¼ c. rye flour
¼ c. long-cooking oats, uncooked
2 T. cornmeal
1 egg white, beaten
2 T. sunflower seeds

Combine yeast and warm water (110 to 115 degrees) in a small bowl; let stand 5 minutes. In a large bowl, combine cottage cheese, honey, egg, oil and salt. Beat at medium speed with an electric mixer until blended. Add yeast mixture and 2 cups bread flour, beating until smooth. Gradually stir in whole-wheat flour, wheat germ, rye flour and oats. Add enough remaining bread flour to make a soft dough. Knead dough on a lightly floured surface until smooth and elastic. Place in a greased bowl; cover and let rise one hour or until doubled in bulk. Punch dough down. Shape into one round loaf and place in a pie plate coated with non-stick vegetable spray and sprinkled with cornmeal. Cover with greased plastic wrap and let dough rise again until doubled in bulk. Brush with egg white and sprinkle with sunflower seeds. Bake at 350 degrees for 35 to 40 minutes. Cool on a wire rack. Makes 6 to 8 servings.

Margaret Scoresby
Mosinee, WI

Cheese Danish Rolls

This scrumptious recipe makes enough for you to share with a crowd…it's sure to be a favorite.

4 c. all-purpose flour
1 c. shortening, melted
1 c. milk
3 eggs, beaten

5 T. sugar
¼ c. butter, melted and divided
Cheese Filling

Combine flour and shortening in a large bowl; mix until crumbly. Heat milk to 120 to 130 degrees. Stir together milk and remaining ingredients except butter; add to flour mixture. Stir 4 to 5 minutes or until dough no longer sticks to the bowl. Refrigerate 3 to 4 hours or overnight. Divide dough into 4 equal parts; roll out each on a floured surface into 11"x7" rectangles. Spoon Cheese Filling down the center of each rectangle; roll up jelly-roll style, starting at short side. Pinch seams together. Arrange on 2 greased baking sheets; brush with 2 tablespoons melted butter. Bake at 375 degrees for 15 to 20 minutes or until golden. Remove from oven; brush with remaining melted butter. Cool and slice. Makes 4 rolls (10 to 12 servings each).

Cheese Filling:

4 (8-oz.) pkgs. cream cheese,
    softened
3 eggs, beaten

1½ c. sugar
2 t. vanilla extract

Beat together all ingredients until thick and pudding-like. Makes 6 cups.

Diane Vasil
Plano, TX

We made these cheese rolls to sell as a fundraiser for our church. It was a wonderfully fun time for women to gather in the kitchens for the day, cooking, talking and watching the children play together.

Diane

Casserole Onion Bread

Pair a wedge of this savory bread with a big bowl of your favorite soup.

1 c. milk
3 T. sugar
1½ T. butter
¾ c. water

1 pkg. active dry yeast
1½-oz. pkg. dry onion soup mix
4 c. all-purpose flour

Heat milk in a saucepan over medium heat just until boiling. Pour into a medium bowl; add sugar and butter. Cool slightly. Heat water until warm (110 to 115 degrees); add yeast and stir until dissolved. Pour yeast mixture into milk mixture; add soup mix and flour. Stir to blend 2 minutes. Cover bowl with a clean tea towel; let rise 45 minutes or until doubled in bulk. Stir dough down; beat vigorously 30 seconds. Turn into a greased 1½-quart casserole dish. Bake, uncovered, at 375 degrees for 45 to 55 minutes. Tent with aluminum foil if top is browning too fast. Cool in pan on a wire rack 5 minutes; turn upside-down to remove and cool on wire rack. Serves 8 to 10.

Grace-Marie Hackwell
Gambier, OH

Bishop's Bread

This is such a pretty bread...and not too sweet. Tasty year 'round!

1½ c. all-purpose flour
1½ t. baking powder
¼ t. salt
6-oz. pkg. semi-sweet chocolate
    chips
1 c. chopped walnuts

1 c. sweetened flaked coconut
10-oz. jar maraschino cherries,
    drained and halved
3 eggs, beaten
1 c. sugar

In a large bowl, sift together flour, baking powder and salt. In a separate bowl, mix together chocolate chips, walnuts, coconut and cherries; add to dry ingredients. In a mixing bowl, beat eggs together with sugar; stir into flour mixture, blending well. Spread batter evenly in a greased and floured 9"x5" pan. Bake at 325 degrees for one to 1½ hours. Wrap in aluminum foil and serve the next day. Makes one loaf.

Kay Demaso
Rever, MA

Honey Koek Loaf

A nice, easy-to-make Dutch bread...kids love it!

2 c. all-purpose flour
1 c. sugar
1 t. cinnamon
½ t. ground ginger
½ t. nutmeg
½ t. ground cloves

1 t. baking soda
½ t. baking powder
½ t. salt
½ c. honey
1 c. boiling water

Combine first 9 ingredients in a large bowl; mix well. Add honey and boiling water; stir together. Pour batter into a greased 9"x5" loaf pan. Bake at 350 degrees for one hour. Cool in pan 10 minutes; turn loaf out of pan and cool on a wire rack. Makes one loaf.

Tawnia Hultink
Ontario, Canada

Apple-Brie Braid

Remember to set out the bread dough the night before to thaw.

2 T. butter, melted and divided
4 c. Granny Smith apples, cored, peeled and chopped
½ c. brown sugar, packed and divided

3 T. chopped almonds
1-lb. loaf frozen bread dough, thawed
4-oz. pkg. Brie cheese, cubed
¼ c. raisins

Pour one tablespoon butter in a skillet; add apples. Sauté 10 minutes; stir in ¼ cup brown sugar. Cook 5 minutes; remove from heat. Stir in almonds; set aside. Roll dough out into a 15"x12" rectangle on a floured surface; place on a greased baking sheet. Spread apple mixture lengthwise down the center of the dough; arrange Brie on top of apples. Make diagonal cuts 1½ inches apart on both long sides of dough to within 1½ inches of filling; alternately fold strips over filling with each strip overlapping. Cover; let rise in a warm place (85 degrees), away from drafts, 1½ hours. In a bowl, combine remaining butter and brown sugar; brush over loaf. Sprinkle with raisins; lightly press into dough. Bake at 350 degrees for 30 minutes. Serves 8.

Jo Ann
Gooseberry Patch

Perfect Lemon Bread

Topped with a lemony glaze, this sweet bread has a refreshing taste.

1½ c. all-purpose flour
1⅓ c. sugar, divided
1 t. baking powder
½ t. salt
2 eggs

½ c. milk
½ c. oil
1½ t. lemon zest
4½ T. lemon juice

Mix together flour, one cup sugar, baking powder and salt in a large bowl; set aside. Beat together eggs, milk, oil and zest; add to flour mixture. Stir until well blended. Pour into a greased and floured 9"x5" loaf pan. Bake at 350 degrees for 45 to 50 minutes. Combine lemon juice and remaining sugar in a small saucepan over medium heat; cook and stir until sugar is dissolved. Using a skewer, poke holes in hot bread; drizzle hot glaze over top and cool. Makes one loaf.

Nichole Martelli
Alvin, TX

terrific tablecloths

Search out fun retro tablecloths at flea markets and tag sales…they're often found for a song. Buy a bunch…they'll bring a burst of color and whimsy to table settings!

Maple Nut Twist

Cinnamon and maple syrup mixed with chopped walnuts make the perfect pairing in this beautifully braided bread.

½ c. milk
½ c. butter, divided
1 pkg. active dry yeast
¼ c. warm water
⅓ c. plus 3 T. sugar, divided
1½ t. salt
2 eggs, beaten
3¼ to 3½ c. plus 2 T. all-purpose
    flour, divided

½ c. brown sugar, packed
½ c. chopped walnuts
¼ c. maple syrup
½ t. cinnamon
½ t. maple extract
1 c. powdered sugar
1 to 2 T. water

In a saucepan, heat milk and ¼ cup butter until butter is melted. In a large bowl, dissolve yeast in warm water (110 to 115 degrees); add 3 tablespoons sugar, salt, eggs and 2 cups flour; beat until smooth. Blend in milk mixture. Add 1¼ to 1½ cups flour until dough forms; knead until smooth. Cover and let rise in a warm place (85 degrees), away from drafts, 2 hours or until doubled in bulk. In a medium bowl, combine brown sugar, walnuts, remaining sugar, maple syrup, ¼ cup softened butter, remaining 2 tablespoons flour and cinnamon; set aside. Punch dough down and divide in half; roll out each half into a 14"x8" rectangle. Spread walnut filling over each rectangle. Starting at long side, roll up dough jelly-roll style. With a sharp knife, cut down the center of the jelly-roll lengthwise; twist 2 pieces together to form a rope braid. Turn ends under and shape braid into a ring. Place dough in a greased 9" pie plate and let rise in a warm place one hour or until doubled in bulk. Bake at 350 degrees for 30 minutes or until golden. Mix together remaining ingredients; drizzle glaze over warm bread. Serves 16 to 20.

Gay Snyder
Deerfield, OH

Every year, I make a special plate of this bread for the neighbors. I had to skip a year due to a birth in my family, and they sure let me know how much they missed it!

Gay

Orange Marmalade Bread

Keep several loaves of this sweet favorite on hand to serve when friends drop by.

½ c. butter or margarine, softened
½ c. brown sugar, packed
2 eggs
10-oz. jar orange marmalade
2¾ c. all-purpose flour

2 t. baking powder
½ t. baking soda
1 t. salt
½ c. orange juice
½ c. chopped nuts

Beat together butter and sugar until light and fluffy. Add eggs, one at a time, mixing well. Blend in marmalade; set aside. Combine flour, baking powder, baking soda and salt; add to butter mixture alternately with orange juice; stir in nuts. Pour into a greased and floured 9"x5" loaf pan. Bake at 350 degrees for about one hour or until a toothpick inserted in center comes out clean. Cool 15 minutes before removing from pan. Makes one loaf.

Linda Behling
Cecil, PA

the right mix

For the most tender loaves and muffins, don't overmix…combine the batter until just moistened. A few lumps won't matter.

Butterscotch Bread

Toss in some sweetened-dried cranberries if you'd like...you just can't go wrong with this recipe!

4 c. all-purpose flour
1½ t. baking powder
1 t. baking soda
½ t. salt
2 c. brown sugar, packed

2 c. buttermilk
2 eggs
3 T. butter, melted
1 c. golden raisins
1 c. chopped pecans

Combine first 8 ingredients in a large mixing bowl; beat at low speed with an electric mixer 2 to 3 minutes. Stir in raisins and pecans; spoon into 2 greased 9"x5" loaf pans. Bake at 350 degrees for 40 to 50 minutes. Let cool in pans 10 minutes; remove from pans to cool completely. Makes 2 loaves.

Mari Courtney
Lewisville, TX

Molasses Buns

Sweet & spicy...you'll want more than one!

½ c. boiling water
½ c. butter, melted
½ c. molasses
½ c. sugar
2 t. baking soda

½ t. ground cloves
½ t. cinnamon
½ t. nutmeg
3 c. all-purpose flour

Mix together all ingredients except flour; set aside until cool. Stir in flour; let stand 20 minutes. Roll dough into balls by tablespoonfuls; place on greased baking sheets. Flatten balls with a spoon; bake at 375 degrees for 20 minutes. Makes about 20 buns.

Patsy Leaman
Crockett, TX

Old-Timey Drop Doughnuts

These unbelievably mouth-watering pastries taste so much better than store-bought doughnuts!

2 eggs
1 c. sugar, divided
1 T. shortening, melted
1 c. milk
1 t. vanilla extract

3½ c. all-purpose flour
2 t. baking powder
⅛ t. salt
½ t. cinnamon
oil for deep frying

In a mixing bowl, beat eggs until light and fluffy; blend in ½ cup sugar, shortening, milk and vanilla. Set aside. Combine flour, baking powder and salt in a separate mixing bowl; stir into egg mixture to make a soft dough. Mix together cinnamon and remaining sugar; set aside. Heat several inches of oil to 365 degrees in a deep saucepan. Drop dough into hot oil by teaspoonfuls, a few at a time. Fry until doughnuts turn themselves over and are golden on all sides. Drain on paper towels; roll in cinnamon mixture while still warm. Makes 3 dozen.

Sharon Crider
Junction City, KS

Old-Time Milk Toast

Popular in the early 1900s with children and those who were feeling under the weather, this recipe remains a delicious comfort food.

2 slices bread, toasted
2 t. butter, softened
1 c. milk

1 t. sugar
⅛ t. nutmeg

Spread toasted bread with butter and place in a shallow bowl. Gently heat milk, sugar and nutmeg in a small saucepan over low heat; stir until sugar dissolves. Pour over toast; let stand until toast swells up and absorbs milk mixture. Serve warm. Serves 2.

Kathy Grashoff
Fort Wayne, IN

Kit's Herbed Bread
(pictured on page 309)

You can also use the herbed butter to dress up grilled corn on the cob, fresh veggies and warm rolls.

6 T. butter, softened
2 T. fresh parsley, minced
2 green onions, finely chopped
2 t. fresh basil, minced

1 clove garlic, minced
¼ t. pepper
1 loaf French bread, halved
    lengthwise

Combine all ingredients except bread in a small bowl; mix well. Spread on cut sides of bread. Place bread on an ungreased baking sheet. Broil 4 inches from heat for 2 to 3 minutes or until golden. Keep refrigerated for up to 2 weeks or store in the freezer for one month. Serves 8.

Nola Coons
Gooseberry Patch

My friend, Kit, makes this all the time.

Nola

Mom's Sweet Potato Biscuits

Mom's Sweet Potato Biscuits

Serve these biscuits with ham...delicious!

2 c. self-rising flour
3 T. brown sugar, packed
¼ t. cinnamon
⅛ t. allspice
3 T. shortening

¼ c. plus 2 T. butter, divided
1 c. canned sweet potatoes,
    drained and mashed
6 T. milk

Combine flour, brown sugar and spices; cut in shortening and ¼ cup butter with a fork until crumbly. Add sweet potatoes and milk, stirring just until moistened. Turn dough out onto a floured surface and knead several times. Roll out dough to ½-inch thickness on a floured surface; cut with a 2-inch round biscuit cutter. Place biscuits on an ungreased baking sheet. Melt remaining butter; brush over biscuits. Bake at 400 degrees for 10 to 12 minutes or until golden. Makes about 1½ dozen.

Nancy Wise
Little Rock, AR

Melt-In-Your-Mouth Biscuits

Split and serve with butter and jam or topped with sausage gravy.

1½ c. all-purpose flour
½ c. whole-wheat flour
4 t. baking powder
½ t. salt
2 T. sugar

¼ c. chilled butter
¼ c. shortening
⅔ c. milk
1 egg, beaten

Sift together flours, baking powder, salt and sugar; cut in butter and shortening. Add milk; stir in egg. Turn dough out onto a floured surface and knead several times. Roll out to ½-inch thickness. Cut with a biscuit cutter; place biscuits on ungreased baking sheets. Bake at 450 degrees for 10 to 15 minutes. Makes one to 2 dozen.

Sherri Hagel
Spokane, WA

Strawberry Surprise Scones

These are wonderful, light scones with strawberry jam inside!

My family enjoys these and my kids get a kick out of eating them.

Marla

1 c. all-purpose flour
1 c. whole-wheat flour
3 T. sugar, divided
1 T. baking powder
¼ c. butter, sliced
⅔ c. milk
1 egg, beaten
⅓ c. strawberry jam

In a large bowl, combine flours, 2 tablespoons sugar and baking powder. Cut in butter until mixture resembles coarse crumbs. Stir in milk and egg until just combined. Turn dough out onto a floured surface and knead about 4 times until dough just holds together. Divide dough in half. Roll out one half into an 8-inch circle and place on a greased baking sheet. Spread jam on top of dough, leaving a one-inch border. Roll out remaining dough into an 8-inch circle and place on top of jam. Press edges lightly to seal; sprinkle with remaining sugar. Cut into 8 wedges, but do not separate. Bake at 425 degrees for 20 minutes. Makes 8 scones.

Marla Arbet
Burlington, WI

Chocolate Scones

For a tasty variation, use white chocolate chips instead of milk chocolate…even add some dried cherries or blueberries.

1 c. sour cream or buttermilk	1 t. salt
1 t. baking soda	1 c. butter
4 c. all-purpose flour	1 c. milk chocolate chips
1 c. sugar	1 egg, beaten
2 t. baking powder	1 T. vanilla extract
¼ t. cream of tartar	Garnish: additional sugar

Combine sour cream or buttermilk and baking soda in a small bowl; set aside. In a large bowl, combine flour, sugar, baking powder, cream of tartar and salt. Cut in butter with a pastry blender; stir in chocolate chips. Add egg and vanilla to sour cream mixture; stir into dry ingredients just until moistened. Turn dough out onto a floured surface; roll or pat out dough into a round about ¾-inch thick. Cut into wedges or cut out circles with a large, round cookie cutter. Place on greased baking sheets; sprinkle with additional sugar, if desired. Bake at 350 degrees for 12 to 15 minutes or until golden. Makes about one dozen.

Terry Parke
Indianapolis, IN

goodies to go

Share your homemade goodies with a friend. Wrap scones in a tea towel and tuck them into a basket along with a jar of jam. A sweet gift that says, "I'm thinking of you!"

Blue Cheese Cut-Out Crackers

You'll love these delicate cheese wafers with a touch of hot pepper!

1 c. all-purpose flour
¼ c. plus 3 T. butter, softened
¼ c. plus 3 T. crumbled blue
    cheese
½ t. dried parsley

1 egg yolk
¼ t. salt
4 t. whipping cream
¼ t. cayenne pepper

    Mix all ingredients together; let rest 30 minutes. Roll dough out onto a floured surface to about ⅛-inch thickness. Use your favorite spring cookie cutter shapes (flowers, teacups, wedding bells) to cut out the crackers. Place on ungreased baking sheets; bake at 400 degrees for 8 to 10 minutes or just until golden. Cool completely on baking sheets. Carefully remove the delicate crackers when cool. Makes 1½ to 2 dozen.

party perfect

Snap up stoneware butter crocks when you find them at flea markets. They're just the right size for serving party spreads and dips, as well as butter.

Lighter-Than-Air Potato Rolls

These are wonderful right out of the oven, served with butter, jam, apple butter or honey.

½ c. instant mashed potato
    flakes
1 t. sugar
2 T. butter, softened

½ c. hot water
⅓ c. cold water
2 c. biscuit baking mix

Combine potato flakes, sugar, butter and hot water. Stir in cold water and baking mix. Turn dough out onto a floured surface and knead 8 to 10 times. Roll out dough into a 10"x6" rectangle. Cut into 12 squares; place on an ungreased baking sheet. Bake at 450 degrees for about 10 minutes. Makes one dozen.

Linda Cuellar
Riverside, CA

sweet butter

Bring along the sweetest pats of butter to serve with Lighter-Than-Air Potato Rolls. Butter slices cut with mini cookie cutters or pressed with cookie stamps make it easy to be creative.

Old-Fashioned Icebox Rolls

This is also a good dough to use for making cinnamon rolls.

1 pkg. active dry yeast
¼ c. warm water
½ c. boiling water
⅓ c. shortening
⅓ c. sugar

½ c. cold water
½ t. salt
1 egg, beaten
3¾ c. all-purpose flour

In a small bowl, combine yeast and warm water (110 to 115 degrees); let stand several minutes. In a large bowl, combine boiling water, shortening and sugar. Add yeast mixture, cold water, salt, egg and flour. Mix and knead until smooth. Cover and refrigerate overnight. Form into golf ball-size balls and place in a greased 13"x9" baking pan. Cover; let rise in a warm place (85 degrees), away from drafts, until doubled in bulk. Bake at 400 degrees for 12 to 18 minutes or until golden. Makes 2 dozen.

Muriel Gundy
Morley, MI

A very old tried & true recipe from my mother and aunt.

Muriel

Fiesta Cornbread

If you'd like, shred Pepper Jack cheese and substitute for the Cheddar...it will add more kick!

1 c. cornmeal
1 c. buttermilk
8-oz. can creamed corn
2 jalapeño peppers, chopped
½ t. salt
¾ t. baking soda

2 eggs, beaten
1 small onion, chopped
¼ c. oil
1 c. shredded Cheddar cheese,
    divided

    Combine first 8 ingredients; set aside. Heat oil in an 8- to 10-inch cast-iron skillet; pour in half the batter. Sprinkle with half the cheese; pour remaining batter over top. Sprinkle with remaining cheese; bake at 400 degrees for 30 minutes. Serves 6 to 9.

Kathryn Harris
Lufkin, TX

Honey-Corn Muffins

Savor these muffins on a chilly day with a steamy pot of tea...sweetened with honey, of course!

1 c. yellow cornmeal	¼ c. corn
¼ c. all-purpose flour	¼ c. honey
1½ t. baking powder	3 T. butter, melted
1 egg, beaten	Honey Butter
⅓ c. milk	

Combine cornmeal, flour and baking powder; set aside. In a separate bowl, combine egg, milk, corn, honey and butter. Add egg mixture to cornmeal mixture, stirring just enough to moisten. Fill paper-lined muffin cups ⅔ full. Bake at 400 degrees for about 20 minutes. Serve with Honey Butter. Makes 9 to 12 muffins.

Honey Butter:

1 lb. butter, softened	8-oz. jar honey

Combine butter and honey; whip until smooth. Spoon into a covered container; keep refrigerated.

Lisa Ann Panzino DiNunzio
Vineland, NJ

Lemon-Raspberry Crumb Muffins

The secret to these flavorful favorites is the lemon zest.

2¼ c. all-purpose flour, divided
½ c. plus ⅓ c. sugar, divided
2 t. baking powder
½ t. baking soda
½ t. salt
8-oz. container lemon yogurt

½ c. oil
1 t. lemon zest
2 eggs
1 to 1½ c. raspberries
2 T. butter

*These are the
BEST muffins!*

Linda

In a large bowl, combine 2 cups flour, ½ cup sugar, baking powder, baking soda and salt. In a small bowl, combine yogurt, oil, lemon zest and eggs. Add to dry ingredients; stir just until dry ingredients are moistened. Gently stir in raspberries. Coat muffin cups with non-stick vegetable spray and fill ¾ full. Combine remaining flour and sugar; cut in butter with a pastry blender or fork until crumbly. Sprinkle topping over batter. Bake at 400 degrees for 18 to 20 minutes. Makes one dozen.

Linda Hendrix
Moundville, MO

anytime treat

Serve up freshly baked muffins anytime! Place muffins in a freezer bag and freeze. To warm frozen muffins, wrap in heavy foil and pop into a 300-degree oven for 12 to 15 minutes.

Grandma's Chocolate
Cake, page 298

divine desserts

Enjoy a sweet ending to your meal with this melt-in-your-mouth collection of delicious desserts. Satisfy your sweet tooth with Miss Lizzie's Pound Cake (page 293). From Chocolate Truffle Cookies (page 267) to Mom's Blackberry Crisp (page 285), you'll find that perfect dessert for family get-togethers, a neighborhood potluck or just about any occasion.

Turtle Cookies

Ideal for placing in a lined vintage picnic tin...any hostess will love these cookies!

18½-oz. pkg. chocolate fudge
   cake mix
1 T. water
2 T. oil

2 eggs
8-oz. pkg. pecan halves
Chocolate Frosting

Combine dry cake mix, water, oil and eggs; mix well and set aside. Arrange pecans in clusters of 3 on greased baking sheets; reserve any leftover pecans for another recipe. Shape dough into one-inch balls; center one ball on each cluster of pecans and flatten slightly. Bake at 375 degrees for 8 to 10 minutes. Let cool; spread with Chocolate Frosting. Makes about 2 dozen.

Chocolate Frosting:

1 T. oil
2 T. baking cocoa
½ t. vanilla extract

1 c. powdered sugar
2 T. milk

In a bowl, combine oil and cocoa. Add vanilla; add sugar and milk alternately to make a consistency good for spreading.

Cheri Emery
Quincy, IL

Chocolate Truffle Cookies

You'll love every bite of this oh-so rich favorite...a real chocolate lover's cookie!

1¼ c. butter, softened	1 t. vanilla extract
2¼ c. powdered sugar	2¼ c. all-purpose flour
⅓ c. baking cocoa	12-oz. pkg. semi-sweet
¼ c. sour cream	chocolate chips

Blend together butter, powdered sugar and cocoa. Mix in sour cream and vanilla; add flour and mix well. Stir in chocolate chips. Chill one hour. Form dough into one-inch balls; arrange 2 inches apart on ungreased baking sheets. Bake at 325 degrees for 15 minutes or until set. Cool at least 10 minutes on wire racks. Makes 2 dozen.

Angie Biggin
Lyons, IL

flavor fun

Give your favorite chocolate recipe a delectable cherry flavor...simply replace the vanilla extract with almond extract.

Double Peanut Butter Cookies

Enjoy these soft, chewy, peanut-buttery cookies warm from the oven.

1½ c. all-purpose flour
½ c. sugar
½ t. baking soda
¼ t. salt
½ c. shortening

¾ c. creamy peanut butter,
  divided
¼ c. light corn syrup
1 T. milk

Combine flour, sugar, baking soda and salt. Blend in shortening and ½ cup peanut butter until mixture resembles coarse meal. Blend in syrup and milk. Form into a roll 2 inches thick; chill at least 30 minutes. Cut into ⅛-inch- to ¼-inch-thick slices. Arrange half the slices on ungreased baking sheets; spread each with ½ teaspoon peanut butter. Top with remaining slices; seal edges with a fork. Bake at 350 degrees for 12 minutes or until golden. Makes about 2 dozen.

Shari Miller
Hobart, IN

sweet bundle

Tie a stack of 3 big cookies together with a length of jute and arrange them in the middle of a dinner plate or inside a lunchbox for a sweet surprise!

In the late 1960s, when I was in the first grade, I got an Easy-Bake Oven for Christmas...I was so excited! My friend and neighbor, Joe, would come over and for hours on end we would bake and bake. Years later, after we had outgrown the oven, Mom had a yard sale... in it was my oven, just waiting for another little girl to have and enjoy.

Shari

Chocolate Chip Cookies

Three types of chips are mixed into these delicious little gems…they are unbelievably yummy!

I LOVE these cookies! I know you will, too.

Christi

1½ c. butter
1 c. brown sugar, packed
1½ c. sugar
4 eggs
1 T. vanilla extract
1 t. lemon juice
3 c. all-purpose flour
1¼ t. salt
2 t. baking soda

½ c. long-cooking oats,
   uncooked
2 (6-oz.) pkgs. chocolate chips
6-oz. pkg. English toffee
   baking bits
6-oz. pkg. peanut butter chips
2 c. chopped walnuts
1 t. cinnamon

In a large bowl, beat butter, sugars and eggs at medium speed with an electric mixer 5 minutes. Add vanilla and lemon juice; add flour, salt and baking soda. Stir in remaining ingredients. Drop by tablespoonfuls 2 inches apart onto a lightly greased baking sheet. Bake at 325 degrees for 15 minutes. Makes 8 dozen.

Christi Miller
New Paris, PA

Washtub Cookies

This recipe's unusual name comes from the fact that with all the ingredients, you just might need a bowl as big as a washtub to mix them all up in!

1 c. shortening
½ c. butter
2 c. sugar
1¾ c. brown sugar, packed
⅓ c. molasses
4 eggs, beaten
2 t. vanilla extract
1 c. crunchy peanut butter
3 c. all-purpose flour

6 c. quick-cooking oats,
   uncooked
2 t. baking soda
1 t. salt
2 t. cinnamon
½ t. nutmeg
½ t. ground ginger
½ t. allspice
1½ c. peanuts, chopped

Combine shortening, butter, sugar, brown sugar, molasses, eggs, vanilla and peanut butter in a very large mixing bowl. Beat at medium speed with an electric mixer just until blended; set aside. In another very large bowl, combine remaining ingredients; add to shortening mixture. Mix until well blended. Drop by tablespoonfuls 2 inches apart onto lightly greased baking sheets. Bake at 350 degrees for 8 to 10 minutes; cool on wire racks. Makes 6 dozen.

Joyce LaMure
Reno, NV

Chocolate-Mint Brownies

Be sure to make plenty...these won't last long!

4 (1-oz.) sqs. unsweetened baking chocolate, divided	½ c. all-purpose flour
¾ c. butter, divided	1 c. powdered sugar
1 c. sugar	1 to 2 T. cream or milk
2 eggs, beaten	½ t. peppermint extract
	3 drops green food coloring

In a medium saucepan over low heat, melt 2 squares chocolate with ½ cup butter. Remove from heat; stir in sugar. Add eggs and mix again. Blend in flour and mix well. Pour into a greased 13"x9" baking pan; bake at 350 degrees for 15 minutes. To prepare frosting, combine powdered sugar, 2 tablespoons butter, cream to desired consistency, peppermint extract and green food coloring. Spread frosting on brownies; refrigerate one hour. Melt remaining chocolate with remaining butter; drizzle over green frosting. Refrigerate 30 minutes; cut into squares when firm. Makes 2 dozen.

The Best Blondies

For an extra-special dessert, serve each square topped with a scoop of ice cream and caramel sauce...delicious!

1 c. butter, melted
2 c. brown sugar, packed
2 eggs, beaten
2 t. vanilla extract
2 c. all-purpose flour
½ t. baking powder

¼ t. salt
1 c. chopped pecans
1 c. white chocolate chips
¾ c. toffee or caramel
    baking bits

Line a 13"x9" baking pan with parchment paper. Spray sides of pan with non-stick vegetable spray and set aside. In a large bowl, mix together butter and brown sugar. Beat in eggs and vanilla until mixture is smooth. Stir in flour, baking powder and salt; mix in pecans, chocolate chips and baking bits. Pour into prepared pan and spread evenly. Bake at 375 degrees for 30 to 40 minutes or until set in the middle. Allow to cool in pan before cutting into squares. Makes one dozen.

this takes the cake

If you see a vintage cake pan with its own slide-on lid at a tag sale, snap it up! Not only is it indispensable for toting frosted bar cookies to a party, it also makes a clever lap tray for kids to carry along crayons and coloring books on car trips.

Caramel Fudge Brownies

This recipe starts with a cake mix that makes it super easy to put together.

This recipe came from my very special mother-in-law, and although she's no longer with us, her recipe continues to be a family favorite.

Sue

18½-oz. pkg. German
   chocolate cake mix
¾ c. butter, melted
5-oz. can evaporated milk,
   divided

14-oz. pkg. caramels,
   unwrapped
1 c. semi-sweet chocolate chips

Combine dry cake mix, butter and ⅓ cup evaporated milk. Spread half the mixture into a greased 13"x9" baking pan (this layer will be very thin). Bake at 350 degrees for 12 minutes. Melt caramels and remaining evaporated milk in a microwave-safe bowl on high 3 minutes; stir and set aside. Immediately after removing from oven, sprinkle brownies with chocolate chips; pour caramel mixture over top. Spoon remaining cake batter by heaping tablespoonfuls over chocolate chips; do not mix. Bake at 350 degrees for 15 to 17 minutes. Cut into squares. Makes 2 dozen.

Sue Roberson
Peoria, AZ

Mom's Instant Coffee Bars

These bars are big on flavor! They're loaded with chocolate chips, coffee and cinnamon.

2 c. brown sugar, packed
½ c. butter, softened
2 eggs
3 c. all-purpose flour
1 t. salt
1 t. baking soda
1 t. cinnamon

1 t. instant coffee granules
1 c. boiling water
½ c. chopped nuts
12-oz. pkg. semi-sweet
   chocolate chips
Coffee Frosting

Blend together brown sugar and butter in a large mixing bowl. Add eggs; mix well. Add flour, salt, baking soda and cinnamon. Mix well; set aside. Dissolve coffee in boiling water; stir into mixture. Fold in nuts and chocolate chips. Spread in a greased and floured 13"x9" baking pan. Bake at 350 degrees for 20 minutes. Immediately frost with Coffee Frosting. Cut into squares. Makes 2 to 3 dozen.

Coffee Frosting:

1 c. powdered sugar
1 T. butter, softened

1 t. instant coffee granules
1 T. boiling water

Blend together powdered sugar and butter in a medium bowl; set aside. Dissolve coffee in boiling water; blend into sugar mixture.

Kim Malusky
Twinsburg, OH

I used to love it when my mom would make these. I wasn't old enough to drink coffee, so eating them made me feel "grown up."
Kim

Grandma's Chocolate Popcorn

Pop up a batch of this tasty treat and your family will demand more…it's addictive!

14 c. popped popcorn
3 c. crispy rice cereal
Optional: 2 c. dry-roasted
   peanuts

1½ lbs. melting chocolate,
   chopped
3 T. creamy peanut butter

In a large bowl, combine popcorn, cereal and peanuts, if desired; set aside. Combine chocolate and peanut butter in a microwave-safe bowl. Microwave on high 2 to 3 minutes or until melted, stirring after every minute. Pour over popcorn mixture, tossing to coat well. Spread onto a large greased non-stick baking sheet; cool completely. Break apart; store in an airtight container up to 5 days. Makes about 20 to 22 cups.

Jayne Kohler
Elkhart, IN

I always helped my grandma make this great snack when I stayed at her house…now my kids really love it, too!

Jayne

care package

A mini mailbox of goodies makes a terrific treat for a faraway friend. Fill the mailbox with packets of candy-striped stationery and envelopes, stamps, cookies, candies and gift mixes. Tuck in a phone card so you can catch up on holiday plans!

Cashew Brittle

No candy thermometer is required for this quick & easy candy.

¼ c. unsalted butter
2 c. sugar
1 c. light corn syrup

2 c. dry-roasted salted cashews
1½ t. baking soda

    Combine first 3 ingredients in a heavy saucepan. Bring to a boil; brush down sides with water and a pastry brush. Continue to boil, stirring constantly, 5 to 6 minutes or until mixture is lightly golden. Stir in cashews. Cook an additional minute, swirling pan to prevent nuts from burning. Stir in baking soda. Pour mixture onto a greased baking sheet. Spread to make an even layer. Let cool completely. Break into pieces. Makes about 2¼ pounds.

Ruth's Caramels

These soft & delicious candies are great for gift-giving.

This recipe was given to me by a very sweet lady, Sister Ruth, who makes these candies for her family every Christmas.

Mel

1 c. butter
16-oz. pkg. brown sugar
⅛ t. salt
1 c. light corn syrup

14-oz. can sweetened
   condensed milk
1 t. vanilla extract

    Melt butter in a heavy saucepan over low heat; add sugar and salt, mixing well. Stir in corn syrup. Gradually add condensed milk, stirring constantly. Cook and stir over medium heat about 12 to 15 minutes, until mixture reaches the firm-ball stage, or 244 to 249 degrees on a candy thermometer. Remove from heat; stir in vanilla. Pour into a greased 9"x9" baking pan. Cool; cut into squares. Wrap in squares of wax paper, twisting at ends. Makes 6 to 7 dozen.

Mel Chencharick
Julian, PA

Mocha Pecan Fudge

For bite-size bon-bons, scoop warm fudge with a mini melon baller. Roll balls in a mixture of powdered sugar and baking cocoa. Mmm!

1 c. chopped pecans
3 (6-oz.) pkgs. semi-sweet
   chocolate chips
14-oz. can sweetened
   condensed milk

2 T. strong brewed coffee,
   cooled
1 t. cinnamon
⅛ t. salt
1 t. vanilla extract

Place pecans in a microwave-safe pie plate. Microwave, uncovered, on high 4 minutes, stirring after each minute; set aside. In a large microwave-safe bowl, combine chocolate chips, condensed milk, coffee, cinnamon and salt. Microwave, uncovered, on high 1½ minutes. Stir until smooth. Stir in vanilla and pecans; immediately spread into a greased aluminum foil-lined 8"x8" baking pan. Cover and refrigerate until firm, about 2 hours. Remove from pan; cut into one-inch squares. Cover and store at room temperature. Makes about 5 dozen.

Samantha Starks
Madison, WI

sweet shapes

A sweet way to give a gift of fudge! Press a cookie cutter into freshly made fudge to fill it completely, lift out (cookie cutter and all) and chill. Wrap in festive cellophane and tie with a sparkly ribbon…sweet!

Martha Washingtons

Martha Washingtons

You'll love this old-fashioned chocolate candy that's chock-full of coconut, nuts and creamy milk...yum!

1 c. butter, melted and cooled
14-oz. can sweetened
    condensed milk
2 c. powdered sugar
2 c. pecans or walnuts, chopped

14-oz. pkg. sweetened
    flaked coconut
20-oz. pkg. melting chocolate,
    chopped

Combine all ingredients except chocolate; mix well and chill overnight. Roll into balls the size of marbles; set on wax paper-lined baking sheets or trays. Melt chocolate in a double boiler. Dip balls into chocolate and return to wax paper to cool. Makes about 6 dozen.

Renee Velderman
Hopkins, MI

Peanut Butter Drops

That's right...only four ingredients to whip up this extra peanut-buttery treat.

½ c. creamy or crunchy
    peanut butter
1 c. milk

2 c. sugar
1 t. vanilla extract

Combine peanut butter, milk and sugar in a large heavy saucepan over medium heat. Cook until mixture reaches the soft-ball stage, or 234 to 243 degrees on a candy thermometer. Add vanilla; beat at low speed with an electric mixer until fudge begins to lose its gloss. Immediately drop by tablespoonfuls onto wax paper-lined baking sheets. Let stand at room temperature until set. Makes about 1½ dozen.

Faith Harris
Orlinda, TN

Cream Puffs

Wow your guests with this creamy pastry. Instant pudding mix makes the filling a cinch to whip up.

1 c. water
½ c. butter or margarine
1 c. all-purpose flour
4 eggs
8-oz. pkg. cream cheese
2 (3½-oz.) pkgs. instant
    vanilla pudding mix

4 c. milk
8-oz. container frozen whipped
    topping, thawed
chocolate syrup to taste

In a saucepan, bring water and butter to a boil; remove from heat. Add flour and beat with a fork until it forms a ball. Place into a mixing bowl; add eggs, one at a time, beating well after each addition. Pour and spread into a 15"x10" jelly-roll pan. Bake at 400 degrees for 25 to 30 minutes; while baking, poke holes with a toothpick in the pastry to let the air out. Let cool. Beat cream cheese at medium speed with an electric mixer; add pudding mix and milk; beat until smooth. Spread mixture evenly over pastry. When ready to serve, spread whipped topping over pudding layer and drizzle with chocolate syrup. Serves 10 to 12.

Jane Granger
Manteno, IL

Scrumptious Strawberry Kabobs

You won't want to miss this oh-so-easy way to enjoy sweet summer strawberries!

12 strawberries, hulled
12 doughnut holes
6 wooden skewers

¼ c. semi-sweet chocolate chips
2 T. butter

Thread berries and doughnut holes alternately on skewers; place on a wax paper-lined baking sheet. In a small saucepan, combine chocolate chips and butter; melt over low heat, stirring until smooth. Drizzle over kabobs. Chill 10 minutes or until set. Makes 6 kabobs.

Sarah Hoechst
Bismarck, ND

summertime grilling

Grilled fruit is a great summertime dessert...try spooning blueberries into pitted peach halves. Sprinkle on a little brown sugar, wrap in aluminum foil and grill until peaches are tender, about 10 minutes.

Mom's Blackberry Crisp

Be sure to heap the berries on because they'll cook down.

¾ c. sugar, divided
¾ c. plus 1 T. all-purpose
    flour, divided
1 t. cinnamon, divided
5 to 6 c. blackberries

⅛ t. salt
⅓ c. butter
¼ c. chopped walnuts
Optional: ¼ t. orange or
    lemon zest

The best crisp I ever had...very simple and quick to make!

Pat

Combine ¼ cup sugar, 4 to 5 tablespoons flour and ½ teaspoon cinnamon; gently fold into berries. Spread in a greased 9" pie plate. Combine remaining sugar, flour and cinnamon; add salt. Cut in butter a little at a time with a fork or pastry blender. Add chopped nuts and zest, if desired. Sprinkle topping over berries. Bake at 400 degrees for about 20 minutes or until golden. Serves 4 to 6.

Pat Gilmer
West Linn, OR

summer goodness

Fresh-picked berries are a special country pleasure. Store them in a colander in the refrigerator to let cold air circulate around them. There's no need to wash them until you're ready to use them.

Sky-High Strawberry Pie

Save a few perfect berries to garnish this delicious pie.

3 qts. strawberries, hulled
   and divided
1½ c. sugar
6 T. cornstarch
⅔ c. water
Optional: several drops red
   food coloring

10-inch deep-dish pie crust,
   baked
1 c. whipping cream
1½ T. instant vanilla
   pudding mix
Garnish: several whole
   strawberries

In a large bowl, mash berries to equal 3 cups; set aside along with remaining whole berries. Combine sugar and cornstarch in a large saucepan. Stir in mashed berries and water; mix well. Bring to a boil over medium heat, stirring constantly; heat and stir 2 minutes. Remove from heat; add food coloring, if desired. Pour mixture into a large bowl; chill 20 minutes, stirring occasionally, until mixture is slightly warm. Fold in remaining whole berries. Pour into prepared pie crust; chill 2 to 3 hours. Place cream and pudding mix in a small mixing bowl; use a hand mixer to whip until soft peaks form. Spread whipped cream mixture around edge of pie or dollop on individual slices. Garnish, if desired. Serves 8 to 10.

Colleen Lambert
Casco, WI

Cathy's Crisp Apple Pie

Use a mixture of Granny Smith & red delicious apples for a great taste combo of tart and sweet.

9-inch graham cracker crust
1 egg yolk, beaten
5½ c. apples, cored, peeled
    and sliced
½ c. sugar
¼ c. brown sugar, packed

3 T. all-purpose flour
¼ t. salt
½ t. cinnamon
¼ t. nutmeg
Optional: 1 T. lemon juice
Crumble Topping

Brush crust with egg yolk. Bake on an ungreased baking sheet at 375 degrees for about 5 minutes or until golden. Set aside. Combine remaining ingredients, omitting lemon juice if apples are very tart; mix well and spoon into crust. Sprinkle evenly with Crumble Topping. Return pie to baking sheet; bake at 375 degrees for about 50 minutes or until filling is bubbly and topping is golden. Let cool; serve at room temperature. Serves 6 to 8.

Crumble Topping:

¾ c. all-purpose flour
¼ c. sugar

¼ c. brown sugar, packed
⅓ c. butter

Mix ingredients with a fork until crumbly.

Annette Isham
Magnolia, DE

This recipe was passed on to me years ago from my best friend Cathy...it is a cherished keepsake of our friendship as well as the VERY BEST apple pie I've ever had.
Annette

the way the cookie crumbles

Try another scrumptious flavor of ready-to-use crumb crust for your favorite pie...vanilla wafer, shortbread and chocolate cookie are all tasty.

Sour Cherry Pie

An intricate lattice pie crust is beautiful, but there's an easier way! Simply lay half the lattice strips across the pie filling in one direction, then lay the remaining strips at right angles. No weaving required!

2 (9-inch) refrigerated pie crusts
4 c. sour cherries, pitted and
    ½ c. juice reserved
1 c. sugar
1 T. all-purpose flour

2½ T. cornstarch
juice and zest of one lime
2 T. butter, diced
1 egg, beaten
2 T. whipping cream

Roll out one crust; place in a 9" pie plate. Wrap with plastic wrap and chill. Roll out remaining crust ⅛-inch thick. Cut as many one-inch-wide strips as possible to make a lattice; cut any leftover crust into leaf shapes with a mini cookie cutter. Place lattice strips and leaves on a parchment paper-lined baking sheet; cover with plastic wrap and chill. Combine cherries and juice in a large bowl. Sprinkle with sugar, flour, cornstarch, lime juice and zest. Toss well and pour into pie crust; dot with butter. Weave lattice strips over filling. Arrange leaves in a decorative pattern on lattice. Whisk together egg and cream; brush over lattice and edges of crust. Bake at 400 degrees for about 50 minutes, shielding crust after 30 minutes, if needed. Cool slightly before cutting. Serves 6 to 8.

Sharon Demers
Dolores, CO

When I was a little girl my father would sing to me, "Can you bake a cherry pie, Sharon girl, Sharon girl?" My reply would always be a giggle and then a big "Nooo!" Well, I can finally make a cherry pie and only wish that my dad were still with us so I could serve him a big piece.

Sharon

easy as pie

Why save pie just for dessert? Invite family & friends for a pie social…everyone brings their favorite pie, and you provide the ice cream and whipped topping.

Sweet Potato Pie

This classic pie is best served with a big scoop of vanilla ice cream.

14½-oz. can sweet potatoes,
    drained and mashed
¾ c. milk
¾ c. brown sugar, packed
2 eggs, beaten
1 T. butter, melted
½ t. salt
½ t. cinnamon
9-inch pie crust

Combine all ingredients except crust in a blender; process until smooth. Pour into pie crust. Bake at 400 degrees for 10 minutes. Cover edges of crust with aluminum foil. Reduce heat to 350 degrees; bake 35 more minutes or until a knife tip inserted in center comes out clean. Serves 6 to 8.

Irene Robinson
Cincinnati, OH

Aunt Elaine's Pink Lemonade Pie

To quickly prepare a homemade graham cracker crust, place 24 graham crackers in a plastic zipping bag and roll them with a rolling pin. Add ¼ cup sugar and 6 tablespoons melted butter.

The recipe for this delicious pie was handed down to us from my husband's great-aunt Elaine. Our daughter even won an award at a dessert competition with this wonderful concoction.

Kathy

6-oz. can frozen pink lemonade
    concentrate, thawed
14-oz. can sweetened
    condensed milk
8-oz. container frozen whipped
    topping, thawed
¼ t. red food coloring
Optional: ¼ to 1 t. lemon
    extract
9-inch graham cracker crust
Garnish: red decorating sugar

Mix lemonade concentrate, condensed milk, whipped topping and food coloring together until well blended. If desired, stir in lemon extract to taste, for a more tart flavor. Pour into crust; sprinkle with decorating sugar, if desired. Cover and freeze 4 hours to overnight. Thaw slightly before serving to make slicing easier. Serves 8 to 12.

Kathy Sharp
Westerville, OH

Mom's Chocolate Pie

This chocolate pie is crowned with a fluffy & golden meringue topping...perfect!

½ c. all-purpose flour
1¼ c. sugar
3 T. baking cocoa
3 eggs, separated and divided
2 c. water

¼ c. butter
⅛ t. salt
1 t. vanilla extract
1 t. butter extract
9-inch pie crust, baked

Combine flour, sugar and cocoa; blend in egg yolks and set aside. In a large saucepan, combine water, butter and salt; heat until butter is melted and let cool slightly. Add flour mixture to water mixture; heat until thick. Let cool; add extracts. Pour into baked pie crust. In a large mixing bowl, beat egg whites at medium speed with an electric mixer until stiff peaks form. Spread meringue over filling, sealing edges carefully. Bake at 350 degrees for 10 minutes or until lightly golden. Serves 6 to 8.

Debbie Driggers
Greenville, TX

This pie was always a holiday tradition in my family. Knowing that my husband loved chocolate pie, my mother always made an extra pie and hid it for him.

Debbie

Miss Lizzie's Pound Cake

A yummy caramel frosting paired with a moist & delicious pound cake makes for an irresistible dessert.

1 c. butter, softened
½ c. shortening
3 c. sugar
¼ t. salt
6 eggs

1 c. milk
1 t. imitation vanilla butter
    and nut flavoring
3 c. all-purpose flour

In a large mixing bowl, beat together butter and shortening at medium speed with an electric mixer; gradually add sugar and salt. Add eggs, one at a time, beating well after each addition; set aside. Combine milk and flavoring; add to butter mixture alternately with flour. Spread into a greased and floured 10" tube pan. Bake at 325 degrees for one hour or until a toothpick inserted in center comes out clean. Remove from pan; cool completely before frosting. Serves 8 to 10.

Caramel Frosting:

1½ c. brown sugar, packed
½ c. sugar
½ c. butter

5-oz. can evaporated milk
1 t. vanilla extract

In a saucepan over medium heat, combine all ingredients except vanilla. Cook 15 minutes, stirring constantly. Remove from heat; stir in vanilla. Immediately spread over cooled cake.

Jody Brandes
Hartfield, VA

This recipe came from my grandfather's neighbor back in the 1950s. I've been making it for forty-five years and topping it with my mom's caramel frosting. I think you'll love it as much as I do.

Jody

egg advice

Eggs work best in baking recipes when they're brought to room temperature first. If time is short, just slip the eggs carefully into a bowl of lukewarm water and let stand for 15 minutes…they'll warm right up.

Coconut Cream Cake

Smooth & creamy...you won't go home with a single slice!

18½-oz. pkg. white cake mix
3 eggs
⅓ c. oil
1 c. water
½ t. coconut extract
14-oz. can sweetened
    condensed milk

15-oz. can cream of coconut
1 c. whipping cream
1 T. sugar
1 c. sweetened flaked coconut

In a large mixing bowl, combine dry cake mix, eggs, oil, water and coconut extract; beat at medium speed with an electric mixer 2 minutes. Pour into a greased and floured 13"x9" baking pan. Bake at 350 degrees for 30 minutes or until a toothpick inserted in center comes out clean. Combine condensed milk and cream of coconut; stir until smooth. With a large fork, poke holes in even rows all over cake; pour milk mixture over top. Refrigerate several hours or overnight. In a large bowl, beat cream at medium speed with an electric mixer until soft peaks form. Add sugar; beat until stiff. Spread over cooled cake; sprinkle with coconut. Serves 24.

Sharon Tillman
Hampton, VA

sweet endings

Desserts are so tempting, you may want to offer a sampler plate for those who just can't decide!

Rich Rum Cake

There can be no holiday without a delectable rum cake! Garnish with fresh orange slices or chopped nuts.

4 eggs, separated
½ c. brown sugar, packed
   and divided
1 c. all-purpose flour
1 t. baking powder
¼ t. salt
⅓ c. butter, melted
1 t. vanilla extract
Rum Sauce

In a large mixing bowl, beat egg whites at medium speed with an electric mixer until stiff; add ¼ cup brown sugar. In a separate mixing bowl, beat egg yolks with remaining sugar; add to egg white mixture. Fold in flour, baking powder and salt; add butter and vanilla. Pour into a greased and floured tube pan; bake at 375 degrees for 25 to 30 minutes. Remove from oven; poke holes in the top of cake with a long skewer. Drizzle Rum Sauce over cake. Serves 10 to 12.

Rum Sauce:

¼ c. butter
1 c. orange juice
½ c. powdered sugar
½ c. rum or ½ c. water plus
   1 T. rum extract

Melt butter in a small saucepan over low heat. Add orange juice and sugar; stir until sugar is dissolved. Add rum and heat through. Makes 2 cups.

Fresh Strawberry Shortcake

When time is short, use split biscuits, cubed angel food cake or waffles for a speedy version of strawberry shortcake.

1 qt. strawberries, hulled
    and sliced
1 c. sugar, divided
2 c. all-purpose flour
4 t. baking powder
¼ t. salt

⅛ t. nutmeg
½ c. butter
½ c. milk
2 eggs, separated
2 c. sweetened whipped cream
Optional: fresh mint sprigs

Gently toss together strawberries and ½ cup sugar; chill. In a large bowl, combine flour, ¼ cup sugar, baking powder, salt and nutmeg; cut in butter until mixture is crumbly. Combine milk and egg yolks; mix well. Add to flour mixture, stirring just until moistened. Divide dough in half; pat into two greased 9" round cake pans. In a small bowl, beat egg whites at medium speed with an electric mixer until stiff peaks form; spread over dough. Sprinkle with remaining sugar. Bake at 300 degrees for 40 to 45 minutes or until golden. Cool 10 minutes before removing from pan to a wire rack. Cool completely. Place one cake layer on a large serving plate; spread with half the whipped cream. Spoon half the strawberries over cream. Repeat layers. Garnish with mint, if desired. Serves 8.

Nancy Ramsey
Gooseberry Patch

No doubt, one of the best things about summer. Our strawberry patch has become so large, I've shared lots of plants, and this recipe, with all our friends & neighbors!

Nancy

Grandma's Chocolate Cake

(pictured on page 264)

A creamy cocoa frosting tops this rich & decadent cake...the ultimate chocolate indulgence!

3 c. all-purpose flour
2 c. sugar
⅓ c. baking cocoa
½ t. salt
2 t. baking soda
2 eggs

2 t. vanilla extract
¾ c. vegetable oil
2 T. vinegar
2 c. cold water
Chocolate Frosting

In a large bowl, combine flour and next 4 ingredients; mix well. Combine eggs and remaining ingredients in a separate bowl. Add egg mixture to flour mixture; mix well. Spread in a greased 13"x9" baking pan. Bake at 350 degrees for 30 to 35 minutes or until a toothpick inserted in center comes out clean. Cool completely before spreading with Chocolate Frosting. Serves 12.

Chocolate Frosting:

⅔ c. butter-flavored shortening
⅔ c. baking cocoa
4 c. powdered sugar

3 t. vanilla extract
¼ c. milk

Mix together all ingredients; blend until smooth.

Regina Wood
Ava, MO

Peanut Butter & Fudge Pudding Cake

Bake a cake in a slow cooker! Kids big & little are sure to want seconds when you serve this cake warm with ice cream…yummy!

½ c. all-purpose flour
¾ c. sugar, divided
¾ t. baking powder
⅓ c. milk
1 T. oil

½ t. vanilla extract
¼ c. creamy peanut butter
3 T. baking cocoa
1 c. boiling water

In a large bowl, combine flour, ¼ cup sugar and baking powder. Add milk, oil and vanilla; mix until smooth. Stir in peanut butter; pour into a lightly greased slow cooker and set aside. Mix together cocoa and remaining sugar; gradually stir in boiling water. Pour mixture over batter in slow cooker; do not stir. Cover and cook on high setting 2 to 3 hours or until a toothpick inserted in center comes out clean. Spoon onto serving plates; serve warm. Serves 6.

Molly Wilson
Rapid City, SD

Grandma & Katie's Frozen Dessert

Grandma & Katie's Frozen Dessert

Refreshing during the summer, or any time of year, this tasty treat can be made ahead of time.

½ c. creamy peanut butter
½ c. light corn syrup
2 c. crispy rice cereal
2 c. chocolate-flavored crispy
    rice cereal

½ gal. vanilla ice cream,
    softened
½ to 1 c. Spanish peanuts,
    coarsely chopped
Garnish: chocolate syrup

Blend together peanut butter and corn syrup in a large bowl. Add cereals; stir until coated. Press into the bottom of an ungreased 13"x9" baking pan. Spread ice cream over cereal mixture; sprinkle with peanuts. Swirl chocolate syrup over top, if desired. Cover with aluminum foil; freeze at least 4 hours before serving. Cut into squares to serve. Serves 15 to 18.

Jennifer Brown
Garden Grove, CA

This used to be my birthday cake every year...I loved it! To this day every time we make this dessert, I think of all those birthday parties in the backyard.

Jennifer

Pecan Cheesecake

If you don't have time to soften the cream cheese, simply zap it in the microwave on high for 15 seconds.

8-oz. pkg. cream cheese,
    softened
½ c. plus ⅓ c. sugar, divided
2 t. vanilla extract, divided

4 eggs, divided
10-inch pie crust
1¼ c. chopped pecans
1 c. light corn syrup

In a bowl, mix together cream cheese, ⅓ cup sugar, one teaspoon vanilla and one egg until smooth. Pour into pie crust. Sprinkle chopped pecans over filling. In another bowl, combine 3 eggs, corn syrup, remaining vanilla and sugar; whisk until smooth. Pour mixture over pecans. Bake at 350 degrees for 50 to 60 minutes or until set and golden. Let cool. Pecans will rise to the top of the cheesecake and will have a layered appearance when cut. Serves 12.

Cinnamon Rice Pudding

Dollop with whipped cream and top with a cherry, just like Mom used to do.

1 c. jasmine rice, uncooked
3 c. milk
½ c. sugar
4-inch cinnamon stick
1 t. vanilla extract
1½ c. whipped cream

Cook rice according to package directions; stir in milk, sugar and cinnamon stick. Bring to a boil, uncovered, over medium heat. Reduce heat and simmer, about 15 to 20 minutes or until thick and creamy, stirring occasionally. Discard cinnamon stick; cool. Stir in vanilla; gently fold in whipped cream. Serve warm or chilled. Serves 4 to 6.

Staci Meyers
Ideal, GA

Chocolate-Mint Dessert

This dessert is beautiful garnished with mint leaves and crushed peppermint sticks.

1½ c. all-purpose flour
¾ c. butter or margarine
⅔ c. chopped pecans
8-oz. pkg. cream cheese
1 c. powdered sugar
1 t. peppermint flavoring
several drops green food coloring
12-oz. container frozen whipped topping, thawed and divided
2 (3½-oz.) pkgs. instant chocolate pudding mix
3 c. milk

In a bowl, combine flour, butter and pecans; press into a greased 13"x9" baking pan. Bake at 350 degrees for 30 minutes. Beat cream cheese, powdered sugar, peppermint flavoring, food coloring and about ⅔ of the whipped topping. Spread over cooled crust. Combine pudding mix and milk. Pour pudding mixture over cream cheese layer. Spread remaining whipped topping over top. Refrigerate before serving. Serves 12.

Carla Terpstra
Rockport, IL

Grandma Smith's Frostsicles

Enjoy the delicious taste of summertime with these homemade pops.

3-oz. pkg. favorite-flavor
    gelatin mix
.23-oz. pkg. unsweetened
    flavored drink mix

½ c. to 1 c. sugar
2 c. very hot water
2 c. cold water

In a bowl, mix together all ingredients except cold water until completely dissolved. Stir in cold water. Pour into cups or molds and freeze. If freezer pop molds are used, dip molds briefly into warm water for easier removal. Makes 6 to 12.

Lori Crawford
Sebring, FL

keep your cool

Icy treats are always welcome during the long, hot days of summer. For picnic fun, tuck wrapped ice cream sandwiches and other frozen goodies into a pail filled with crushed ice to keep them frosty.

When I was young, my mom made this recipe for us during the hot summer, but never often enough for me as a six-year-old! The "red" flavors...strawberry, raspberry and cherry, were the best. I would sit in the shade on the steps of the front porch, trying hard not to share any drips with the ants. Now I make them for my children, but not often enough, I'm sure.

Lori

Hot Fudge Brownie Sundaes

Homemade brownies, ice cream and hot fudge sauce...can it get any better? Try cutting the brownies with a round cookie cutter just for fun!

¼ c. butter
2 (1-oz.) sqs. semi-sweet
    baking chocolate, chopped
1 egg
½ c. brown sugar, packed
1 t. vanilla extract

¼ t. salt
¼ c. all-purpose flour
4 scoops vanilla ice cream,
    softened
Garnish: chocolate sauce,
    warmed

Combine butter and chocolate in a microwave-safe container; microwave on high until melted, stirring every minute. Stir; cool 10 minutes. In a small bowl, mix together egg, brown sugar, vanilla and salt. Stir into chocolate mixture. Add flour; mix well. Spread batter in an 8"x8" baking pan lined with aluminum foil and sprayed with non-stick vegetable spray. Bake at 350 degrees for 15 minutes or until a toothpick inserted near center comes out clean. Cool completely on a wire rack. Cover; chill until firm. Cut brownies into 8 squares. Spread half with ice cream; top with remaining brownies. Wrap in plastic wrap; freeze overnight. To serve, drizzle with warm chocolate sauce, if desired. Makes 4 sundaes.

Robin Hill
Rochester, NY

ice cream fun

Stock up on ice cream flavors, nuts and toppings...spend an afternoon making banana splits (and memories) with the kids!

Skyscraper Banana Splits

(pictured on page 311)

Big and little kids will line up for these piled-high sundaes!

¼ c. chocolate syrup, divided
4 scoops vanilla ice cream,
    divided
4 bananas, halved lengthwise
    and crosswise

4 scoops chocolate ice cream,
    divided
½ c. strawberry syrup, divided
Garnish: whipped cream

Pour one tablespoon chocolate syrup into each of 4 parfait glasses; add one scoop vanilla ice cream to each. Arrange 4 banana pieces, cut-side out, in each glass; top each with one scoop chocolate ice cream. Drizzle each evenly with strawberry syrup; top each with whipped cream, if desired. Makes 4 banana splits.

Beth Kramer
Port Saint Lucie, FL

Creamy Coffee Granita

(pictured on page 314)

Start this about 3 hours before you'd like to serve it.

6 c. hot, strong brewed coffee
½ c. sugar

Garnish: whipped cream

Pour coffee and sugar into a 13"x9" baking pan, stirring to dissolve sugar. Cover with plastic wrap; place in freezer. Freeze 3 hours, scraping occasionally, until frozen. Serve topped with whipped cream, if desired. Serves 8 to 10.

Root Beer Floats

Make sure your root beer is icy cold so the ice cream doesn't melt too fast!

16-oz. bottle root beer, chilled
   and divided

4 scoops vanilla ice cream,
   divided

Pour ½ cup root beer into each of 4 tall glasses. Add a scoop of vanilla ice cream to each. Carefully pour in root beer to fill each glass to the top. Serves 4.

Virginia Watson
Scranton, PA

Soda Shoppe Chocolate Malts

Have some good, old-fashioned fun and serve these rich treats in antique soda glasses!

8 scoops vanilla ice cream
3 c. milk
4 to 6 T. chocolate syrup

2 t. vanilla extract
¼ c. malted milk powder

Combine all ingredients in a blender. Process until smooth and well blended. Serve immediately. Serves 4.

Jill Burton
Gooseberry Patch

all-occasion menus

pancake breakfast

serves 6

Buttermilk Pancakes (page 91)

Fruity Pancake Topping (page 94)

sausage

coffee

cozy supper

serves 6

*Beef & Broccoli Wellington
(page 146)*

*Glazed Carrots
(page 201)*

Easter celebration

serves 8

Country Glazed Ham (page 13)

**Grand Ma-Ma's Deviled Eggs
(page 14)*

*Country-Style Baked Potato Salad
(page 14)*

*Double recipe.

down-home
comfort

serves 6

Johnny Marzetti (page 69)

mixed salad greens

*Kit's Herbed Bread
(page 251)*

bridal luncheon

serves 8 to 10

Refreshing Mint Punch (page 10)

*Cheese Straws (page 10)

Tea Sandwiches (page 11)

The Best Blondies (page 273)

family night

serves 6

Tamale Pot Pie (page 73)

*Skillet-Toasted Corn Salad
(page 229)*

*Double recipe.

celebrate spring

serves 6

*Blue-Ribbon Ham Casserole
(page 61)*

bakery rolls

**Skyscraper Banana Splits
(page 306)*

*Double recipe.

Independence Day picnic

serves 10

Jen's Pulled Pork (page 141)

coleslaw

Fourth of July Beans (page 17)

Fresh Peach Ice Cream (page 21)

salad supper

serves 4 to 6

Summer Tortellini Salad
(page 221)

crusty French bread

iced tea

breakfast for supper

serves 6

*Herbed Salmon Omelets
(page 106)

Fresh Fruit with Creamy Sauce
(page 95)

*Triple recipe.

company's coming

serves 5

Hashbrown-Pork Chop Casserole
(page 60)

Green Bean Bundles
(page 199)

ladies for lunch

serves 6

Golden Chicken Divan
(page 57)

Tangy Tomato Slices
(page 213)

kids love it

serves 8

Chili Crescent Cheese Dogs
(page 146)

Buffalo Potato Wedges
(page 204)

summer supper

serves 8

Three-Cheese Pasta Bake
(page 76)

Creamy Coffee Granita
(page 306)

Sunday dinner

serves 4

Pot Roast & Sweet Potatoes
(page 152)

Sesame Asparagus
(page 196)

winter night warm-up

serves 10

Chicken Fajita Chowder
(page 189)

Fiesta Cornbread
(page 261)

METRIC EQUIVALENTS

The recipes that appear in this cookbook use the standard U.S. method for measuring liquid and dry or solid ingredients (teaspoons, tablespoons, and cups). The information in the following charts is provided to help cooks outside the United States successfully use these recipes. All equivalents are approximate.

METRIC EQUIVALENTS FOR DIFFERENT TYPES OF INGREDIENTS

A standard cup measure of a dry or solid ingredient will vary in weight depending on the type of ingredient.
A standard cup of liquid is the same volume for any type of liquid. Use the following chart when converting standard cup measures to grams (weight) or milliliters (volume).

Standard Cup	Fine Powder (ex. flour)	Grain (ex. rice)	Granular (ex. sugar)	Liquid Solids (ex. butter)	Liquid (ex. milk)
1	140 g	150 g	190 g	200 g	240 ml
¾	105 g	113 g	143 g	150 g	180 ml
⅔	93 g	100 g	125 g	133 g	160 ml
½	70 g	75 g	95 g	100 g	120 ml
⅓	47 g	50 g	63 g	67 g	80 ml
¼	35 g	38 g	48 g	50 g	60 ml
⅛	18 g	19 g	24 g	25 g	30 ml

USEFUL EQUIVALENTS FOR LIQUID INGREDIENTS BY VOLUME

¼ tsp	=							1 ml	
½ tsp	=							2 ml	
1 tsp	=							5 ml	
3 tsp	=	1 tbls			=	½ fl oz	=	15 ml	
		2 tbls	=	⅛ cup	=	1 fl oz	=	30 ml	
		4 tbls	=	¼ cup	=	2 fl oz	=	60 ml	
		5⅓ tbls	=	⅓ cup	=	3 fl oz	=	80 ml	
		8 tbls	=	½ cup	=	4 fl oz	=	120 ml	
		10⅔ tbls	=	⅔ cup	=	5 fl oz	=	160 ml	
		12 tbls	=	¾ cup	=	6 fl oz	=	180 ml	
		16 tbls	=	1 cup	=	8 fl oz	=	240 ml	
		1 pt	=	2 cups	=	16 fl oz	=	480 ml	
		1 qt	=	4 cups	=	32 fl oz	=	960 ml	
						33 fl oz	=	1000 ml	= 1 liter

USEFUL EQUIVALENTS FOR DRY INGREDIENTS BY WEIGHT

(To convert ounces to grams, multiply the number of ounces by 30.)

1 oz	=	₁⁄₁₆ lb	=	30 g
4 oz	=	¼ lb	=	120 g
8 oz	=	½ lb	=	240 g
12 oz	=	¾ lb	=	360 g
16 oz	=	1 lb	=	480 g

USEFUL EQUIVALENTS FOR LENGTH

(To convert inches to centimeters, multiply the number of inches by 2.5.)

1 in	=		=	2.5 cm		
6 in	=	½ ft	=	15 cm		
12 in	=	1 ft	=	30 cm		
36 in	=	3 ft	= 1 yd	=	90 cm	
40 in	=		=	100 cm	=	1 meter

USEFUL EQUIVALENTS FOR COOKING/OVEN TEMPERATURES

	Fahrenheit	Celsius	Gas Mark
Freeze Water	32° F	0° C	
Room Temperature	68° F	20° C	
Boil Water	212° F	100° C	
Bake	325° F	160° C	3
	350° F	180° C	4
	375° F	190° C	5
	400° F	200° C	6
	425° F	220° C	7
	450° F	230° C	8
Broil			Grill

index

My Favorite Recipes

entrées

frostings, fillings & toppings

Our Story

Back in 1984, we were next-door neighbors raising our families in the little town of Delaware, Ohio. We were two moms with small children looking for a way to do what we loved and stay home with the kids too. We shared a love of home cooking and making memories with family & friends. After many a conversation over the backyard fence, **Gooseberry Patch** was born.

We put together the first catalog & cookbooks at our kitchen tables and packed boxes from the basement, enlisting the help of our loved ones wherever we could. From that little family, we've grown to include an amazing group of creative folks who love cooking, decorating and creating as much as we do.

Hard to believe it's been over 25 years since those kitchen-table days. Today, we're best known for our homestyle, family-friendly cookbooks. We love hand-picking the recipes and are tickled to share our inspiration, ideas and more with you! One thing's for sure, we couldn't have done it without our friends all across the country. Whether you've been along for the ride from the beginning or are just discovering us, welcome to our family!

Your friends at Gooseberry Patch

Find us here too!

Join our **Circle of Friends** and discover free recipes & crafts, plus giveaways & more! Visit our website or blog to join and be sure to follow us on Facebook & Twitter too.

Join our Circle of Friends

VIDEOS

Find us on Facebook

Read Our Blog

Follow us on twitter

www.gooseberrypatch.com